Towns and Villages
OF ENGLA

C000021345

ALCESTER

Towns and Villages
OF ENGLAND

ALCESTER

DAVID GREEN

ALAN SUTTON

First published in the United Kingdom in 1993
Alan Sutton Publishing Limited
Phoenix Mill · Far Thrupp · Stroud · Gloucestershire

First published in the United States of America in 1993
Alan Sutton Publishing Inc · 83 Washington Street · Dover NH 03820

British Library Cataloguing in Publication Data

A catalogue record for this book is available from the British Library

Library of Congress Cataloging in Publication Data applied for

Typeset in 11/13 Bembo.
Typesetting and origination by
Alan Sutton Publishing Limited.
Printed in Great Britain by
Hartnolls, Bodmin, Cornwall.

Contents

Foreword

No historical account of an ancient town like Alcester can ever be exhaustive. When the centuries have yielded so rich a tapestry of interwoven facts, embracing every facet of human life and endeavour, it would require a weighty tome indeed in which to attempt to record in any detail even a digest of the full story. Anything less, of necessity, has to be selective, offering a broad picture which nevertheless reflects the fascination of the underlying historical minutiae.

In thus presenting this account of Alcester's past, I am especially indebted to the Alcester and District Local History Society whose authoritative documentary records have proved a valuable source of reference, and whose photographic collection has provided most of the illustrations. I also acknowledge with gratitude the willing assistance I received from the society's president, G. Edward Saville, during my researches.

David Green

CHAPTER ONE

The Alcester the Romans Knew

Someone once described Alcester as the town which never grew up. This was meant in no derogatory sense, but alluded to the fact that although, over the centuries, there have been numerous factors which so easily could have set this historic little town on a path towards the sort of urban development which has overtaken many other places, Alcester has consistently shrugged them off.

Set in the still largely unspoilt countryside of westernmost Warwickshire, the town marks the spot where the waters of the rivers Alne and Arrow meet, to flow together for a few more meandering miles before joining Shakespeare's Avon near Salford Priors.

To the north, beyond a slim but reassuring green belt, lies the sprawling conurbation of Redditch whose boundaries have nudged ever further outwards since it acquired New Town status in the 1960s. A couple of miles to the west, beyond the little Spittle Brook, the raised spine of the ancient Ridgeway forms a natural boundary between Warwickshire and Worcestershire.

Although it is generally accepted that Alcester's origins date back to the days of the Romans, there is in fact a sufficient amount of evidence to indicate that settlements of one kind or another existed here considerably earlier. When work was being carried out on the town's sewerage system in the 1920s, for instance, two early human skulls were unearthed, male and female, and these were said to be of Neolithic origin.

Remains of flint tools and weapons from the same period have also been discovered, together with fragments of crude pottery and bones from the animals which would have been used for food. One rare example of Neolithic man's considerable ability in fashioning stone, is a beautifully preserved axe head found some years ago at Alcock's Arbour on the outskirts of Alcester.

Bronze Age man evidently knew the area too, and so did his Iron Age successor who left his mark in the form of pottery relics discovered in the vicinity of present-day Meeting Lane.

In these prehistoric times, the whole of this area of Midland England would have been covered by a dense forest in which roamed wolves and other

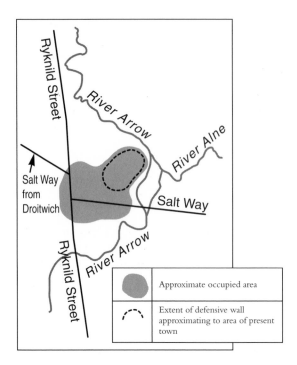

Roman Alcester

wild animals. It is not difficult, therefore, to conjure up pictures of early man creating clearings in which to settle and hunt, unwittingly leaving evidence of his day to day activities.

Some of these settlements may have been used as permanent homes, particularly those on higher ground, while others could well have been temporary sites during hunting expeditions, but there is no doubt, as aerial photographic surveys have shown, that the history of man's occupation of the area in which Alcester now lies, certainly goes back a good deal further than the Romans.

But it is, of course, to the Roman occupation that Alcester really owes its origin. They called it Alauna, according to the majority of historians, although there is one school of thought which confusingly suggests that Alauna was a village in Oxfordshire. Such a possibility is hotly contested in the Alcester of today, where the name of Alauna Avenue firmly confirms the link for all to see.

There is no doubt at all, though, that the modern name of Alcester is derived from that of the River Alne, with the suffix 'cester' denoting the fact that the place was a Roman settlement. This explanation has, in fact, been evident in all the many versions of the town's name which have occurred over the centuries, ranging from Alencestre, Alnecestria and Aucestre, to Alcetur,

Awcetre, Alceter and finally Alcester, with numerous subtle variations along the way.

Even today, although the spelling of the name has settled on the familiar 'Alcester', its pronunciation is a constant source of doubt among a surprisingly large number of people, whose inelegant variants raise more than a few local eyebrows. Let there be no more confusion. Alcester, in the right circles, is pronounced 'Awlster', although with the influence of a little touch of local dialect, 'Awster' is no less acceptable.

For the Romans, with their straightforward Alauna, no such problems presumably existed. It was a name which would have been widely known among their occupying forces, for the town was a strategic station on one of their major lines of communication, Ryknild Street. This joined the great Fosse Way to the south, thus providing a link between the important town of Corinium – the modern Cirencester – and Wall in Staffordshire, sited on Watling Street, the Romans' main road from London to the North-West. Crossing Ryknild Street at the point where Alcester now stands was another important communication artery linking the salt town of Droitwich with the Fosse Way to the east.

Alauna was thus in a significant location, and the importance of its role both as a military station and later as a civilian settlement has gradually emerged during the extensive and painstaking archaeological excavations which have taken place during the present century. These have investigated not only the remains of roads and military and civilian buildings, but the sites of cremations and burials, and as much as possible of the infrastructure of this important Roman settlement.

A large proportion of this work has had to be undertaken in advance of building and development schemes, in order to save and record as much evidence as possible, but it is sadly inevitable that Alcester will keep much of its great treasure-chest of Roman secrets hidden away beneath the surface, probably for all time.

Alcester's Roman origins have, of course, been realised for many centuries. As long ago as the early sixteenth century, the historian John Leland, describing Alcester as a 'praty market towne', said that it 'hath bene a great thinge', adding that 'many tokens of buyldings and bones of men be found'.

In those days, the archaeological significance of such finds would not have been generally recognised, and it was not until the early years of the present century that serious excavation work started to take place.

From the evidence so far discovered, it appears that the Romans first arrived here in about AD 47, some four years after their invasion of Britain. They built a fort to accommodate a detachment of soldiers, and the site of

Archaeologists uncover further evidence of the Roman town near present-day Gas House Lane. (Warwickshire Museum)

this, at Primrose Hill just to the south of the present town, can still be discerned from the air.

It is likely that they built a second fort some years later, nearer a crossing-place over the River Arrow in the vicinity of the modern Bleachfield Street, as the remains of military equipment have been found here. This second stronghold would, in all probability, have been part of the measures taken to counter the uprising led by the intrepid Queen Boadicea, who, not surprisingly, took great exception to the fact that her lands were being systematically occupied by these upstart Roman invaders.

It seems probable that this second fort was the nucleus from which the town developed, as it would have provided a ready source of trade for local settlers earning a living off the land, and would have attracted others to come here to sell their wares and services to the Roman soldiers.

Gradually a small community was established, and this then grew rapidly into a town of some regional importance, even though most of the soldiers garrisoned here would have been moved on, probably around AD 75, in order to help conquer northern Britain.

A male skeleton discovered beneath the site of the Roman Wall. As burials were only permitted in official cemeteries, this unfortunate man may have met his death by accident during the wall's construction, and his body left here. (Warwickshire Museum)

Alcester at that time came within the administrative district of the Dobunni tribe based some 40 miles away at Cirencester. Because of the distance involved, it is possible that the town assumed the role of a seat of local government, or at least a regional communications centre. There is certainly evidence to suggest that by about AD 200, the place was of a considerable size by Roman standards, covering well over 70 acres and supporting a population of at least two thousand.

The Roman town appears to have been mainly sited slightly to the south of the present town centre, although there is also evidence that the area now occupied by the High Street, the parish church and the surrounding roads, was enclosed by defensive earthworks, probably around the end of the second century. Later, these were strengthened into a more substantial town wall.

There is a theory, too, that at some point during their occupation, the Romans may have diverted the River Arrow from a course on the west side of the town, to its present course to the east. This would have presumably been done to make their building operations easier. Another suggestion is that the river was diverted due to natural causes, and that this occurred considerably earlier than the Roman occupation, probably around 500 BC.

A wintry River Arrow near the point where it is joined by the Alne. Oversley Bridge is in the background. It was a settlement on this river confluence which first attracted the Romans to this part of Warwickshire

Archaeological research is not conclusive, but it has certainly unearthed part of a former watercourse on the west side of the town, not far from the present Old Rectory in Butter Street. It all serves to highlight the difficult problems of obtaining and accurately explaining the available evidence in a built-up area such as the centre of Alcester.

But despite these problems, excavations have brought to light a fascinating picture of what life would have been like in Roman times. Judging by the large number of coins and pieces of jewellery so far discovered, it was a place of some wealth. This is also borne out by the wide diversity of buildings which are known to have existed, certainly towards the end of the Roman occupation.

Initially, many of the buildings would have been constructed of timber, with walls of wattle and daub, and roofs of thatch. Some would have been of a circular design, common before the Romans arrived, but these soon gave way to the more substantial rectangular structures favoured by the Roman builders. Gradually, stone was introduced, at least for the foundations, although some of the more prosperous and important inhabitants would have had houses built entirely of stone. For the really wealthy, there were villas with mosaics and wall paintings, tiled roofs, and hypocausts providing the very latest in under-floor central heating.

The Roman town's economic prosperity depended to a large extent on the products of the land, although agriculture was by no means the only trade offering employment to local people. There is evidence of tanning and of bone and bronze work, and there would have been blacksmiths as well as a large number of building workers. There were probably pottery makers here too, although much of the pottery which has so far been discovered, appears to have come from elsewhere in Britain, or was brought across from the continent.

General market traders also seem to have flourished, and there was at least one market area on the site of the modern-day road known as Birch Abbey. All this trade inevitably necessitated an increasing use of the coinage which the Romans had introduced, and there was also a sophisticated tax-collecting system. Some of these taxes would have been paid in produce rather than cash, and for this purpose a building of considerable size, a sort of Roman Inland Revenue office, would have been required. Alcester could well have possessed one such building, as evidence of a sizeable warehouse-like structure, possibly a granary, some 120 ft in length, was discovered beneath the site of a modern-day motor dealer in Priory Road.

If the Romans knew a thing or two about building and town planning, they also brought with them a certain culinary expertise which would undoubtedly have impressed the native Britons. New cooking methods from

These oak piles, excavated by county archaeologists near the site of the present Gateway supermarket, were part of the Roman defensive wall. (Warwickshire Museum)

the continent were introduced, and the Roman *mortarium*, a sort of food processor resembling a pestle and mortar, would have been found in most kitchens worth their name.

A whole variety of new herbs was introduced, and if the evidence uncovered in Alcester is any indication, the average dinner menu could well have been an elaborate affair comprising beef, pork, lamb and poultry, various cereal products including bread, and a range of seasonal garden produce which even included asparagus. There is also local evidence to show that oysters were part of the Roman diet, a delicacy presumably brought in from towns on the coast, or possibly from the continent. All in all, appetites were seemingly well satisfied in Alcester, and if the Roman equivalent of Egon Ronay ever existed, he would have been more than impressed.

Apart from the relics one would expect to find in any Roman town, such as weapons, artefacts, cooking utensils, jewellery, pottery, coins and human remains, Alcester has also yielded other valuable information about this important era in its history through the scientific study of pollen, plant seeds, and even the remains of insects.

Roman furniture, for instance, was no less immune to woodworm infestation than ours is today, and one of the more unusual finds, as recently as

1965, was a bedbug which met its demise in the warmth of an Alcester bed in the second century. The discovery of the oldest known bedbug in Britain, has to be one of Alcester's more bizarre claims to archaeological fame.

No one knows for certain when Alcester's days as a Roman town finally came to an end. Like the rest of Roman Britain, it depended for its prosperity and stability on an economic and monetary system which the Romans had gradually established during the four centuries of their occupation. Suddenly, and for reasons which are obscure, this system appears to have collapsed around AD 400. By then many of the Roman troops had been recalled to help with the defence of their own country, and in about AD 410, the year generally considered to mark the end of the Roman occupation, the emperor Honorius effectively told the Britons to get on with their own lives and if they wanted defending, to do it themselves.

The effect on Alcester was dramatic. The importance of the town's role as a market and centre of administration diminished rapidly, the population declined, a process which may well have been hastened by a plague, and those who were left probably moved into the area within the existing defensive ramparts, in order to consolidate their community.

Alcester's fortunes during the next few hundred years are a matter of conjecture. It is probable that the local Britons still lived and worked here, but whether or not the Saxons settled in the town is not known for sure. However, a small number of excavated Saxon relics and burial sites would seem to indicate some sort of settlement, and there was an important Saxon cemetery at Bidford only 4 miles away.

An account of an ironworks flourishing in Alcester during the eighth century could well be true, as there was abundant timber available in the nearby Forest of Arden, and ore could have been transported from the area we now know as the Black Country.

The smiths labouring at the ironworks were the subject of one of Alcester's more extraordinary stories which appeared in *The Chronicle of Evesham Abbey* written in about 1100. It concerned the life of St Egwin, Bishop of Worcester, who founded Evesham Abbey in the eighth century. It seems that Egwin visited Alcester on a sort of missionary tour, but it was impossible for his preaching to be heard because of the noise created by the smiths at work. This singular lack of piety brought swift retribution. The unfortunate smiths were engulfed in an earthquake, and the iron trade dwindled into non-existence.

This splendid story, apocryphal in part at least, may well confirm the presence of early iron-working in Alcester, but mention of an earthquake was almost certainly introduced to provide some sort of explanation for the deteriorating Roman remains which would have still been visible throughout much of the town.

The centre of Alcester as it was in 1948. Much of this area was originally within the Roman town's defensive wall

A Roman milestone commemorating the Emperor Constantine (AD 306–37), excavated in the Birch Abbey area in 1966

If there is any element of truth in the story at all, it at least suggests that some sort of community existed at Alcester in Saxon times, but there is little else, either documentary or archaeological, to go on. Evidence that the Danes were in the vicinity does exist though, as they apparently founded a settlement in the area now known as Alcester Heath.

Even William I's mammoth nationwide survey of 1086, the Domesday Book, is little help as far as Alcester is concerned, as, rather surprisingly, it contains no mention of the town whatsoever. One explanation for the omission is that Alcester may well have been included under the entry for Bidford, which by that time had assumed considerable regional importance.

Whatever the reason, the fact remains that this particular period of Alcester's history is something of a mystery, and it is not until the arrival on the scene of a Norman nobleman called Ralph de Boteler that an authentic story starts to emerge.

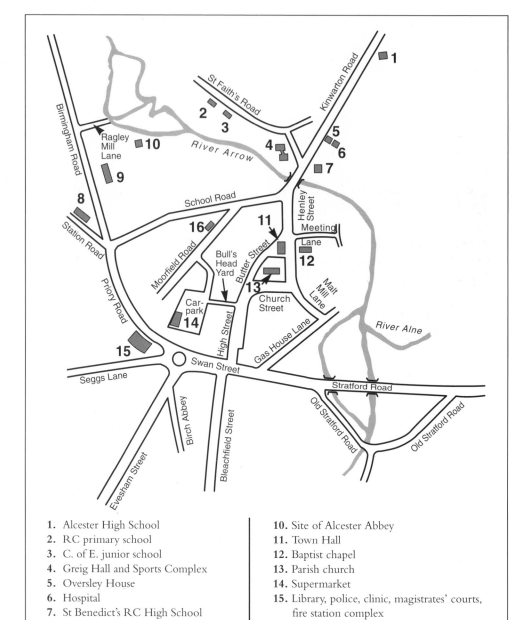

1. Alcester High School
2. RC primary school
3. C. of E. junior school
4. Greig Hall and Sports Complex
5. Oversley House
6. Hospital
7. St Benedict's RC High School
8. The former Minerva needleworks
9. Alcester Grammar School
10. Site of Alcester Abbey
11. Town Hall
12. Baptist chapel
13. Parish church
14. Supermarket
15. Library, police, clinic, magistrates' courts, fire station complex
16. Infants' school

Alcester

CHAPTER TWO

Abbey, Court Leet and a Punctual Sunday Lunch

Ralph de Boteler was a builder on the grand scale. In the early 1100s he built a castle just to the south of Alcester at Oversley, and in about 1140 he founded a Benedictine abbey to the north of the town. The abbey's dedication, by its all-embracing nature, was seemingly intended to ensure as trouble-free an existence as possible. The list of dedicatees included the Holy Trinity, the Blessed Virgin, St Anne, St Joseph, St John the Baptist, St John the Evangelist, and (presumably to cover any important omissions) All Saints.

Not surprisingly, this unwieldy name soon became abbreviated, and the abbey's more popular description was the Church of Our Lady of the Isle. The island in question was formed by the River Arrow which looped round it on it is north and east sides, and by a connecting moat which completed the circle to the south and west.

Boteler's castle has long since disappeared, although what is thought to have been its original site can still be discerned. The abbey, too, has gone, but at least it is possible to pinpoint the position it once occupied between the River Arrow and the present Birmingham road.

The many endowments settled on the abbey by its founder included the chapel associated with his nearby castle, and also the early church which then existed in Alcester itself. But the abbey was never one of the most influential in the land. In fact, the records show that over the centuries it led an extremely chequered existence and was frequently the source of all kinds of trouble for the church authorities. So much for all those precautionary dedications!

On one occasion, the servants of a visiting archbishop were attacked by an unruly gang from Alcester, and on another occasion the incumbent abbot was summoned to appear before Edward III for some unrecorded misdemeanour. There are also records of indiscipline, brawling, poor government, negligence, wastage and debt, but somehow the abbey continued to survive. By 1466, however, the situation had deteriorated to such an extent that Edward IV decreed that the abbey should be taken over by its larger neighbour at Evesham, and Alcester's last abbot resigned. The final ignominy came when the abbey was reduced in status to a priory, a mere cell administered by Evesham, and this remained the situation until the establishment was suppressed, along with so many others up and down the country, during the reign of Henry VIII.

Today, all that is left of the old monastery is hidden below ground, although for many years the nearby main road to Birmingham continued to be known as Abbots Lane and Abbey Street. The present names of Priory Road and Abbey Close are just about the only reminders left.

Alcester's non-appearance in the Domesday Book means that little, if anything, is known about its status as a manor in those formative years of the eleventh century. There seems little doubt that it was a royal manor, but nothing is known of the lord who would have held it.

The first documented evidence of a Lord of the Manor of Alcester comes from the twelfth century, when Sir Robert Corbet received the estate from Henry I, and thus began an association with some of the great families of the Midlands which has continued up to modern times.

Corbet had two daughters, one marrying into the Fitzherbert family and the other into the Boterells, and the manor, having been divided into two parts, descended through these two families. Towards the end of the thirteenth century, the influential Walter de Beauchamp purchased the Fitzherberts' half which his family continued to hold until the middle of the fifteenth century, when Sir John Beauchamp – later created Lord Beauchamp of Powick – bought the other half from the Boterells.

Archetypal Victorians: Mr and Mrs Frazer Brown lived at Beauchamp Court in the second half of the last century. Their home, which still exists, took the name of the original Beauchamp Court, seat of the Lords of the Manor until the seventeenth century

The third Fulke Greville, Lord of the Manor from 1606 to 1628, who gave £300 towards the building of the Town Hall

The Beauchamps were now lords of the entire manor, a situation which was short-lived because when Sir John's son Richard married, the union only produced female offspring, leaving no direct male line to succeed. One of his daughters eventually married Robert, Lord Willoughby de Broke, who again only left female heirs. It was one of these, Elizabeth Willoughby, who married Sir Fulke Greville in 1536, thus bringing the Manor of Alcester into a powerful family, later to become Earls of Warwick, who retained it right up until the last century. In 1813, the manor was bought by the Marquess of Hertford, whose family, the Seymours of noble Ragley Hall on the edge of Alcester, have held the manorial title ever since.

Alcester's former manor-house was Beauchamp Court, which at the time of the Beauchamp occupancy was evidently an impressive dwelling with its own private chapel. When the Grevilles arrived (confusingly, the first three Greville Lords of the Manor were all called Fulke) the building was beginning to show its age. It was the first of the Fulkes, holding the office from 1536 to 1559, who decided to enlarge and restore Beauchamp Court by using stone and other materials from the disused Alcester Priory, an operation which effectively hastened the demise of the old monastic building.

Today, like the Priory, Beauchamp Court has also disappeared. Despite the work carried out by the first Fulke, it eventually fell into ruin when the third Fulke finally moved out in the seventeenth century to take up residence in

Warwick Castle. Today, its site can still be traced by the remains of the original moat, while its name is perpetuated through that of a nineteenth-century farmhouse nearby.

Under the manorial system, it was customary for lords to maintain special courts by which their manors were administered. This was usually done through a Court Baron, a body which met at regular intervals to deal with problems arising from such matters as tenancy and property rights. Certain manors were also allowed to hold a more senior Court Leet, and the Manor of Alcester, because of its regional importance, was one of these. The Alcester court's origin is believed to date back at least to the late thirteenth century.

As Alcester was a trading centre with charters to hold its own markets and fairs, the Court Leet was a necessity. It met twice a year and dealt with a wide range of matters which included the framing and enforcement of local bye-laws, the preservation of the peace, and the maintenance of fair trading in food, drink and other merchandise.

In order to carry out these varied duties, the Court Leet depended on a formidable list of elected officers, including a High and Low Bailiff; constables; fish, flesh and ale tasters; leather-sealers; bread-weighers; and others with equally specific responsibilities. In short, they were a cross between our modern trading standards officers and the police force, and as such they kept a wary eye on the behaviour of citizens and traders alike, particularly on market days.

The Court Leet's High Bailiff in 1902 reads the proclamation of Edward VII from a window of the Town Hall

Alcester's Court Leet flourished as an integral part of local life until well into the second half of the seventeenth century, by which time the powers of the parish rather than the manor were beginning to exert themselves. The role of the parish was, by then, an important factor in local administration throughout the country, and records show that, as a result, the influence of the old Court Leet in Alcester was diminishing rapidly. It seems to have continued its operations somewhat half-heartedly for a few more decades, and probably petered out altogether in the following century.

Then, in the 1780s, for reasons which presumably were pressing at the time, it appears to have been revived in a new form, embracing both Court Leet and Court Baron, and meeting every few weeks rather than twice a year as in the past. Alcester, it seemed, was in dire need of stricter administration, and the revived Court was there to ensure it was carried out.

This new-found enthusiasm was fairly short-lived, however, and by the 1820s the Court Leet was losing its last vestiges of authority. Most of its duties were taken over once and for all by the parish, and its customary requirement to appoint constables was eventually superseded when an Act of Parliament led to the formation of a professional county police force.

But the Court Leet did not entirely disappear. It has lived on, without any

The historic Court Leet, at one time exercising far-reaching jurisdiction over the town's affairs, still perpetuates an ancient tradition princpally in a ceremonial role. This photograph was taken in the 1980s

real authority, as a colourful reminder of an ancient tradition, and even survived an Act of Parliament as recently as 1977 which officially abolished most of the country's remaining Courts Baron and Courts Leet. The reason for its unlikely survival was that Alcester was named as one of very few exceptions to the 1977 Act, and thus the Court still legally exists to this day as a delightful anachronism in a modern world. Its officers are still dutifully elected, even though their traditional roles are now essentially ceremonial, adding a colourful touch of history to the life of the town.

Although Alcester's earliest buildings have long since disappeared, and are consequently only known through documented records, their legacy often lives on. Even the old Roman town has, to a large extent, influenced the size and shape of modern Alcester, as the present town centre roughly coincides with the area which was originally enclosed within the encircling town wall.

Even though no signs of the old wall remain above ground, the more observant among present-day shoppers will know that the course of a small section of it has been delineated by a swathe of red tarmac which curves across the town's main car park outside a modern supermarket. A similarly coloured area close by denotes the former site of the Roman settlement's granary or storehouse.

The medieval church which formed one of the endowments when Ralph de Boteler founded Alcester Abbey has also disappeared, although by its very existence, it is historically linked, over the centuries, with the parish church of St Nicholas which stands on the same site and serves Alcester today.

The early church met with some sort of disaster in the 1720s. There may have been a fire; the structure may have succumbed to the effects of time and weather; it may even have suffered damage at the hands of Puritan vandals during the periods of religious turmoil in the previous century. There are no clear records of exactly what happened. What is known for certain, is that the old church had to be virtually rebuilt, and only the lofty fourteenth-century tower was retained.

The original church mainly comprised a chancel, a nave, two side aisles, and of course the tower. Each of the aisles fulfilled the function of a chantry chapel with its own priest, and they were independently dedicated, one to Our Lady and the other to All Saints. The former was founded in about 1286 by the same de Boteler family who founded the abbey, while the Beauchamps of Beauchamp Court founded the latter in the fourteenth century.

The church was therefore, in a sense, three separate places of worship, a fact which has led to the erroneous assumption on the part of some historians, that Alcester could once boast three parish churches.

Both chantries were eventually closed under Henry VIII's vindictive programme of dissolution, but not before the one dedicated to Our Lady had

The original Newport's Free School at Birch Abbey, forerunner of the present-day Alcester Grammar School

been set on a course which was to provide another of those legacies from which the town is still benefiting to this day.

In about 1490 it was moved from within the church to a new building by the road now known as Birch Abbey, where it doubled as a school for local boys. It continued as a school after it was deprived of its religious role, enjoying an endowment of £20 a year from a local benefactor named Walter Newport. Thus it became known as Newport's Free School which, in the course of time, developed into the prestigious Alcester Grammar School standing today by the side of the road to Birmingham.

The old Newport's Free School building survived until the 1960s when it was unceremoniously demolished to make room for a new housing development. But its spirit lives on in the road names in this part of the town – Chantry Crescent, Boteler Close and Newport Drive.

So with the chantries long gone, and the condition of the old church demanding massive restoration, the new building took shape in 1729. Its construction was entrusted to Edward and Thomas Woodward of Chipping Campden, builders and masons of considerable reputation. The building consisted of a nave flanked by Doric columns and two aisles. There was no chancel, as there is today, but instead the Woodwards built an apse to accommodate the altar. The cost of the new church, met partly by donations from other parishes up and down the country, was £1,020, a sum which today would hardly pay for a few yards of scaffolding, but which in 1729 was a not inconsiderable amount.

The interior of the building would have appeared very different from the familiar layout of today. Both the aisles had prominent galleries, and at the west end of the nave was the organ loft. Completely obliterating the view of the altar was a massive three-decker pulpit described as 'hideous' by one parishioner in the last century.

Others must have agreed with the parishioner's opinion, for in 1871 not only was the offending pulpit removed in favour of a less flamboyant Victorian design which is still here, but the apse was replaced by a more conventional chancel with two side chapels. At the same time, the galleries were taken down, and the organ resited in one of the new chapels, now used as a sacristy. All in all, the alterations restored the traditional appearance of a parish church, after a period in which the building must have looked rather like a non-conformist preaching establishment.

Modern-day visitors to Alcester, fascinated by the town's history, inevitably include a tour of the church on their itinerary, for it offers a wealth of interest, as well as a few surprises. The portable communion rail used in the side chapel, for instance, forges an unlikely link between Alcester and Frederick Jackson Land in the deepest Arctic, only a snowball's throw from the North Pole.

Frederick Jackson, an Arctic explorer of the last century, was born in Alcester in 1860. In the last years of the century he embarked upon an expedition which resulted in his proving that Franz Josef Land was not part of a vast polar continent but an archipelago in its own right. It was while he was trudging the Arctic wastes in pursuit of his goal, that he came across the exhausted Norwegian explorer Fridtjof Nansen who was returning from an expedition of his own which had taken him and his party far to the north. Jackson put his ship at Nansen's disposal to enable the Norwegian to return home, thus saving his life. In gratitude, Nansen named the territory north of Franz Josef Land after the man from Alcester. It is an epic story indeed, and one for the good people of Alcester to ponder as they kneel at Jackson's memorial communion rail in their parish church.

An unusual story of quite a different nature is linked with the window in the north wall of the chancel. This features the patron saint of the church, St Nicholas, who stands upon a small tau cross, so named because its shape resembles the Greek letter *tau*. The reason why this particular cross accompanies the saint in the design of the window, is to commemorate a remarkable discovery made in the rectory garden in 1873. An authentic Saxon tau cross made from a walrus tusk was dug up by chance, and after

An engraving depicting the High Street in the middle of the last century. The building on the right occupies the site of the original Bull Ring

expert examination it was said to have originally been the head of a staff. It depicts a representation of the Crucifixion, and such was its immense value, that it was put in the care of the British Museum where it is still a much-prized exhibit.

Opposite this unusual window is another, in the south wall of the chancel, depicting St Faith, a reminder that at one time she, not Nicholas, was the church's patron saint. She appears benevolent enough though, charitably bearing no resentment for her deposition as she eyes her successor across the church.

The building is also notable for its memorials, the most impressive of which is the elaborate alabaster tomb of the first Sir Fulke Greville, Lord of the Manor in the sixteenth century, who lies with his wife, Elizabeth. Sir Fulke not only found the time to undertake the considerable duties of landowner and sheriff of both Warwickshire and Leicestershire, but managed to father no less than fifteen children. All of these are represented round the tomb, dutifully mourning the loss of their prolific parents.

Elsewhere in the church is a fine marble memorial to the second Marquess of Hertford of Ragley Hall, who died in 1822, and another features the seated figure of his kinsman, Sir Hamilton Seymour, whose death occurred in 1880. The Seymours, as we have seen, acquired the lordship of the manor in 1813.

Other treasures in the church include a British Legion triptych remembering the men of Alcester who lost their lives, not only in the two world wars, but in the Korean conflict too, and there is a fascinating benefactions board of the seventeenth century. In complete contrast, on the south wall of the nave, are three colourful modern tapestries of 1985 depicting in elaborate detail the life and times of the people of Alcester and their town.

On the north wall, opposite the tapestries, is an intriguing memorial tablet which can lead to all sorts of wild speculation among those who stop to read it. It commemorates the death of a local butcher named Mander, whose wife evidently died in 1828 after what is described as 'an awful accident'. No further explanation is given, and the nature of the poor woman's demise is left to the mercy of one's imagination.

Those visitors whose interests are mechanical rather than ecclesiastical, unfailingly stop and stare at the old mechanism of the church clock which is

The parish church from the High Street, as it appeared in an engraving of 1847

on view at the back of the nave. It did sterling service from 1682 until the present century, when it was deposed by the modern technology of an electric motor which was installed in its place.

The clock itself has been the cause of many a raised eyebrow among local people and visitors alike, as it is rather awkwardly fixed across the south-west corner of the tower rather than occupying a more conventional position in the centre of one of the walls. The reason for this unusual arrangement has been the subject of much imaginative speculation, but the truth of the matter seems unremarkably obvious. The clock was evidently placed in its strange position so that it faced directly down the High Street and could be easily seen.

Like the new clock mechanism, the eight bells in the church are also modern, having been installed earlier this century to replace the six which were originally cast in 1735. Made by the celebrated John Taylor of Loughborough, they bear some delightful names: St George, Peace, Unity, Concord, Faith, Hope, Charity, and of course St Nicholas.

No longer, though, does one of the church bells perform what was once a decidedly unusual, if useful, function. In days gone by, it was evidently rung at one o'clock on a Sunday to inform the men in the local pubs that their wives had the meal ready. It is tempting to wonder which bell was used for this purpose. Perhaps it was the one called Charity, for the good wives of Alcester would surely have had to exercise this commendable quality towards husbands who persistently needed reminding to come home for their Sunday lunch.

CHAPTER THREE

Troublesome Religion and a Fine Town Hall

The abbey, the parish church and the chantry chapels may have contributed a major chapter to the history of Alcester, but they were certainly not alone in playing a part in the religious evolution of the town.

The dissent which followed the advent of Protestantism after the Reformation, made its mark too, and it was at its height during the years of the Civil War in the seventeenth century.

Alcester was largely in sympathy with the Parliamentarians, if only because it was presumably safer to follow the lead of the Lord of the Manor, who was not only anti-Royalist but a strong supporter of religious dissent. Between Alcester and Worcester to the west, however, the Royalists largely held sway, supported by such influential Catholic landowners as the Throckmortons of Coughton Court.

Thus Alcester not only found itself a fertile breeding ground for the religious dissenters, but in the front line of the warring factions. On one occasion, shortly after the Royalists' spectacular defeat at Naseby in 1645, the king and his troops were retreating towards the friendly territory of Herefordshire, hotly pursued by several thousand Scottish Parliamentarians under the command of Lord Leven, augmented by supporters from Derbyshire. This unruly horde of Roundheads rampaged through Alcester during the chase, and then returned to the town later, after discovering that the bridge over the Severn at Upton was not strong enough to carry so formidable an army.

Such had been the devastation and pillage caused by the ill-disciplined Scots during their advance across the Midlands, that the Parliamentarian Committee for Warwickshire, together with its counterparts from neighbouring counties, met in Alcester to discuss the many complaints which had been made and to agree payments of compensation. This humanitarian contribution to the affairs of the Civil War may only have earned Alcester a passing reference in the history books, but it was a worthy involvement nevertheless.

Meanwhile, the various dissenting religious bodies were establishing themselves in the town, and the Quakers, the Presbyterians and the Baptists were all holding regular meetings here. Even the parish church had a Presbyterian minister, but he soon lost his job after the Restoration of the Monarchy which saw the re-establishment of the Church of England.

The Restoration inevitably meant that the activities of the dissenters were driven underground, and for a time their meetings were held clandestinely, often in the homes of supporters. Initially, the laws against non-conformists of whatever persuasion were repressive to say the least, but eventually each sect was allowed to have its own chapel, and towards the end of the seventeenth century, the existence of the dissenters had become officially recognised and tolerated.

The Quakers, in 1677, were the first to build their own meeting-place in Alcester, on a site behind the east side of the High Street, but it ceased to serve its original purpose in 1835, when it became a private dwelling. It still exists at the end of one of the narrow alley-ways – or 'tueries' as Alcestrians call them – between the present-day shops.

The Presbyterians chose a site off the other side of the High Street, in Bull's Head Yard, and they erected their chapel here in the early 1720s. It operated until 1900, although its existence was dogged by a lack of funds and a declining congregation. For a period it even took the Unitarians under its wing, and for some eleven years after 1882 it closed its doors altogether. Following its final closure in 1900, its contents were disposed of and it was sold into private hands. Even that was not the end of its chequered existence, for the old building eventually became derelict, until a fire in the 1960s finally wiped it off the Alcester map for ever.

The Baptists were less unfortunate. Having originally held their meetings in private dwellings, they were eventually permitted to build a meeting house in the 1730s, in what became known as Meeting House Lane, now more commonly called just Meeting Lane.

This in turn was superseded by a larger place of worship in 1859 on an adjacent site. The latter, facing Church Street, still survives, and its imposing Classical-style frontage is one of Alcester's architectural gems. Its predecessor still exists too, partly hidden behind its grand Victorian successor.

With all this non-conformity now firmly established in Alcester, the Methodists were in no hurry to set their own sights on the town, despite the activities of the Wesleys and their revival of evangelism. It was not, in fact, until 1812 that the Methodists, already well-organised up the road in Redditch, turned their attention towards Alcester, and in that year they converted a cottage in Priory Road into their first chapel in the town. This they later enlarged, and it flourished until the 1960s, when the present modern Methodist church was built in its place.

Part of Priory Road, *c.* 1912. The now replaced Methodist chapel is in the right foreground, and the Roman Catholic church, built in 1889, in the background

Now an integral part of of the town's religious life, the Methodists of today can be thankful that the local townspeople are more tolerant than their predecessors. The records relating to that early chapel in 1812 reveal that on one occasion, a visiting minister had a brick thrown at him while he was preaching, and it nearly cost him his life. On another occasion a minister from Redditch came to the town to spread the word of Methodism, but was set upon by an unruly mob, who dragged him up and down the road and inflicted wounds on him which he carried for the rest of his life.

Meanwhile, the Catholics, who would have worshipped in the parish church until the Reformation, had problems of their own. The majority would have become recusants, refusing to submit to the law which, between the sixteenth and eighteenth centuries, required them to recognise the Church of England. At least some of them would have braved the risk of worshipping at nearby Coughton Court, the historic home of one of the country's great Catholic families, the Throckmortons.

By 1889, however, in a more enlightened world, they were able to build

The parish church of St Nicholas in 1955. The solitary parked car makes dramatic comparison with the traffic-thronged town centre of today

their own church in Alcester, on a site in Priory Road. Dedicated to Our Lady and St Joseph, it is an impressive building harking back in style to the fourteenth century, and incorporating stone appropriately quarried on the Throckmortons' land at Coughton. Architecturally, as well as ecclesiastically, the church today presents a stark contrast to the modern meeting-place built for the Jehovah's Witnesses round the corner in Station Road.

The Anglican parish church of St Nicholas, because of its dominant island site overlooking the High Street, is now Alcester's best-known landmark. But it has not always enjoyed such public prominence, and it is difficult to realise that until the beginning of the last century it was hemmed in by closely-packed shops and houses known as the Shop Row. As a result, Church Street bordering the churchyard, would have been a good deal narrower than it is today, presenting a scene of colourful congestion on market days when this whole area was thronged with the stalls of traders.

On the northern side of the churchyard is another of Alcester's treasured architectural landmarks, with a long and fascinating history. This is the old Market Hall building, or Town Hall as it is now popularly known, in the centre of what was originally the Market Place where once stood the old High Cross.

Its origin dates back to 1618 when the third of the Fulke Grevilles was

Lord of the Manor. By this time he had moved from his Alcester home in Beauchamp Court, and as Lord Brooke, he was living in Warwick Castle. But his interest in the well-being of Alcester had not diminished, and he gave the sum of £300 for the building of a market hall.

In those early days it was a pillared edifice, open at the sides to the elements, but it did offer a degree of protection to some of the market traders. It had no upper floor, as Lord Brooke's £300 was only sufficient for the modest ground-floor building. The additional storey, of timber-framed construction, was not added until 1641, if the date carved on one of the massive roof timbers is any indication.

A little over a century after the upper storey was added, the Lord Brooke of the day, as Lord of the Manor, agreed to forego the tolls on market sales which he had been receiving, on condition that the local people assumed responsibility for the upkeep of the 'Town House and Market Place'. This arrangement seems to have worked well for a time, but by 1874 the old building was beginning to show signs of neglect, and Lord Hertford, who was then the Lord of the Manor, decided to assume responsibility himself.

The Town Hall reverted to manorial ownership, and Lord Hertford had the spaces between the pillars filled in to create an enclosed ground floor, thus giving the building its present-day appearance.

In its long life, the old Town Hall has served many purposes. At one time it accommodated the local lock-up for prisoners awaiting trial by the Court Leet. This tiny cell had just one small window which, although now blocked in, can still be discerned. The building also provided a home for the town stocks and pillory, and for the early manually-operated fire engine which once served the town.

After Lord Hertford carried out his alterations, he leased the building to the county council which used it mainly for petty sessional court purposes, but by 1919, following a public fund-raising appeal, the old hall was acquired once again by the town. This time the idea was to dedicate the building as a memorial to the local men who fell in the 1914–18 war, and it duly became the Memorial Town Hall.

It continues in that role to the present time, and although its days of market trading have long gone, it still serves the town as a popular meeting-place for a variety of public functions. A plaque on the west wall provides a fitting reminder that the ancient building 'was purchased by public subscription from the Lord of the Manor, The Most Honourable The Marquess of Hertford, as a permanent memorial to the brave men of Alcester and Oversley who gave their lives in the Great War of 1914-1918'. The plaque is dated 1919 and bears the names of the two responsible signatories: George Thomas, High Bailiff, and R.H. Spencer, Low Bailiff. It is interesting that inside the Town

The Town Hall seen from Butter Street, *c.* 1910. The original open arches were filled in in 1874

Town Hall and church provide a timeless background for a snowballing skirmish during the harsh winter of 1947

Hall there are boards listing all the town's High and Low Bailiffs since medieval times.

Thus, one of Alcester's oldest surviving buildings provides an emotive link, not only with a human war tragedy of the present century, but with many notable chapters in the town's history stretching back nearly four hundred years. The parked cars which almost encircle it today may appear somewhat obtrusive in the context of its ancient stone and timbering, but it seems to accept their presence benevolently, regarding them perhaps as just another transient manifestation of man's influence on the town it has known for so long.

The Town Hall in the 1950s forms a backcloth for the traditional New Year's Day meet of the local hunt.

CHAPTER FOUR

Bountiful Acres and Burgeoning Trade

With the unrest of the Civil War and the problems of religious dissent behind it, Alcester settled into a period of relative stability. For centuries the town's economy had been largely based on farming, and a large proportion of the local population earned its livelihood either by producing or marketing the products of the land.

The growing of barley supported the local malting industry. Sheep were reared for their wool, which in turn provided work for the local spinners and weavers. Flax was grown for linen production, and the hides of cattle kept the tanners and leatherworkers busy. The meat would have gone to the town's various butchers centred on The Shambles, a small area at the northern end of what is today known as the High Street.

Corn and other food crops were grown too, and so was hemp, a crop which by the early years of the nineteenth century had led to a flourishing rope-making industry in the town.

Evocative legacies of some of these early industries can still be found today in Alcester's road names. Ropewalk, for instance, is one such name, although strangely the road which bears it is some distance from the site of the town's former rope-making workshop. This occupied premises behind what is today No. 31 High Street, and it served the town until just before the First World War. Bleachfield Street recalls the area where linen was laid out for bleaching in the sun, while Malt Mill Lane is a reminder of the once flourishing malting industry.

A fascinating relic of this particular industry is a restored malt kiln in the communal gardens serving the imaginative development of dwellings for the elderly which has been created behind the existing buildings of Malt Mill Lane.

Malting was, in fact, one of the more important of the industries dependent upon a locally-grown crop, and the town supported numerous malthouses, seven of them being recorded in Malt Mill Lane alone. The Old Malthouse, the remarkable jettied timbered building which still graces the corner of Malt Mill Lane and Church Street, is a notable survivor from Alcester's malting days, although it now serves as one of the town's more picturesque shops.

The northern end of Malt Mill Lane as it was in the years following the Second World War

Malting, of course, is closely associated with brewing, and at one time several of Alcester's numerous public houses, only a few of which still exist, would have brewed their own beer. The town also possessed its own Alcester Brewery, which owned and operated a large malt-house in now vanished premises off the western side of Henley Street.

The brewery itself was an impressive Victorian edifice with a lofty brewing tower, situated behind the Baptist Chapel in Meeting Lane. Its beer went almost exclusively to local pubs – tied houses which were not permitted to sell beer from any other brewer – and this arrangement effectively put an end to the town's smaller independent brewing operations.

The Alcester Brewery thrived until the outbreak of the First World War when brewing ceased, and today little evidence remains of the grand buildings which once served to quench the thirsts of so many Alcestrians.

Until the advent of the internal combustion engine, most of the heavier commodities which had to be distributed around the town – like the barley for the malthouses and the brewed beer for the inns – would have been carried in horse-drawn wagons. These, of course, would have provided the necessity for two more of the trades which at one time flourished in the town, the blacksmith or farrier, and the wheelwright. At one time, these craftsmen were as vital to a community as the motor mechanic is today, and most towns and villages would have possessed more than one of each.

Throughout much of the last century, for instance, there were up to four blacksmiths working in Alcester at any one time, and as they also undertook the vital work of horse-shoeing, they were, in effect, farriers as well. By the turn of the century their number had started to decline, and by the early 1930s only one was trading. Even so, he still would have had plenty of horseshoes to fit, despite the increasing number of cars.

The forges used by the blacksmiths were located in various parts of the town, and one which is of particular interest was sited just off Bleachfield Street, not far from The Swan Inn. When it was demolished in the 1970s, a number of documents were discovered relating to a blacksmith who worked there in the early years of the present century, and these are now in the possession of the County Record Office in Warwick.

The blacksmith in question was a Frank Haywood, employed by a local ironmonger named John Elsley, whose shop was at No. 15 High Street. It was

Alcester Brewery, now long disappeared, as it was around the turn of the century

Malt Mill Lane before the First World War. At one time there were seven malt kilns in this one street alone

not uncommon in those days for ironmongering and smithing to be carried on as a joint business. Haywood was evidently a versatile practitioner of his trade, and the time-sheets which were among the records discovered, indicate that he regularly worked exceedingly long hours.

He was apparently kept busy repairing agricultural implements and machinery, and was clearly an accomplished millwright, as he also carried out repair work at the local mills. On one occasion he is reported as having been sent to Ragley Hall to attend to Lord Hertford's private gasworks, and he still seems to have had time to cope with his main occupation, the making and fitting of horseshoes.

Another of Haywood's jobs was to repair and maintain the kitchen equipment at The Globe, the ill-fated hotel which until the 1960s, stood boldly marking the junction of Swan Street and Evesham Street, a site now occupied by an undistinguished traffic island.

The same documents which tell us about the remarkable Frank Haywood, also provide an insight into the ironmongery business run by his employer, John Elsley. It was, by all accounts, a typical example of the sort of all-purpose ironmonger's shop which could be found at that time in towns all over the country. No doubt smelling strongly of paraffin, it stocked tools in abundant

A horse-drawn two-wheeled cart waits outside The Rose and Crown in Evesham Street. This inn was closed in the 1960s

variety, horticultural implements, locks, cutlery, agricultural requisites, hardware, and virtually anything else that one would have expected of a reputable ironmonger. Key-cutting, knife-grinding and tool-sharpening were available too.

Like the other blacksmiths in the town, Frank Haywood would certainly have been called upon to repair the metal parts of the many types of horse-drawn vehicle which were a familiar sight on the streets, like wheel-rims, springs and other fitments. But it was, of course, the job of the wheelwright to make and repair the wheels themselves.

Contemporary directories listing local tradesmen in the last century, refer to several wheelwrights, including the Cooke family who had businesses at various times in Priory Road, Malt Mill Lane and the High Street. Another local wheelwright, with a keen sense of business acumen, was a William Perkins in the 1870s, who, if times were hard, could fall back on his other occupation as landlord of The Three Tuns.

In the early years of the present century, the trade of coach-building was gaining importance, a reflection not only of the continuing demand for horse-drawn transport, but of the increasing number of motor vehicles on

An example of George Clark's coach-building. This horse-drawn delivery van was owned by the local co-operative society

George Clark's coach-building company operated at Arrow during the early decades of the present century. It was a successful operation judging by the size of his work-force

Alcester's roads. The Cooke family of wheelwrights recognised the opportunity and switched to coach-building, while in the neighbouring village of Arrow, a coach-builder named George Clark set up a business producing vehicle bodies of many types which became familiar sights in and around the town.

Leatherworking was also an important trade associated with Alcester, and at one time – particularly in the seventeenth and eighteenth centuries – it played a vital part in the local economy and provided employment for many specialist tradesmen. Some of these, like the tanners, would have handled the raw hides, but many more were engaged in the manufacture of the various products made from leather, including saddles, harnesses, boots and shoes.

Gloves were made in Alcester too, although by the middle of the eighteenth century, the trade was in decline – as was the local leather industry in general – probably because of growing competition from the leather-workers of Worcester, who had already given their city a long-standing reputation as one of the country's major centres of glove-making. The trade, although diminished, did persist in Alcester for a good many years, and old directories show that as late as 1871 there was still one lone Louisa Winfield working as a glove-maker in the town.

The saddlers fared a good deal better, and so did the makers and repairers of boots and shoes. By the middle of the last century there were no fewer than seventeen of the latter trading in the town. But these too diminished in number as the years passed, and by the early 1930s, with manufacturing becoming increasingly centralised, Alcester's boot and shoemakers numbered less than half a dozen.

Among the leading practitioners of the trade at the end of the last century were the Blackband family, who operated from premises on the site of the present modern post office in the High Street. Most of the Alcestrians of today, as they queue up for their postage stamps or pensions, are presumably blissfully unaware that a century ago they would have been standing amongst all the paraphernalia of a busy shoemaking workshop, redolent with the pungent smell of new leather.

Many of Alcester's trades, and certainly those dependent upon arable and livestock farming, would have been reflected in the hustle and bustle of the town's traditional weekly market. This ancient institution owed its existence to charters obtained by lords of the manor dating back as early as 1292. They permitted the holding not only of weekly markets but also regular fairs, which were primarily for trading purposes, although they were also popular social occasions, characterised by various forms of entertainment and general merry-making.

These early fairs are not to be confused with the traditional hiring or mop

A purpose-designed delivery wagon coach-built by George Clark for a local tradesman around the turn of the century

fairs which were not officially authorised until the reign of Elizabeth I. The main purpose of the latter was to provide an opportunity for those seeking work to demonstrate their availability to potential employers – the farmers and gentry – by bearing tokens of their various trades.

The word *mop* may literally have meant what it says, so the housemaid would have carried a mop to indicate her calling. On the other hand, the word could well have been used in its old English context, meaning a tuft. Thus a shepherd seeking work would have worn a tuft of wool and hopefully attract the attention of a visiting farmer who needed extra help with his flock.

Alcester still holds its mop fair every October, although the hiring element died out towards the end of the last century. Nowadays it is a colourful mixture of street stalls and entertainment and a high spot in the town's annual calendar. The old market custom is perpetuated too, and the traditional summer street market is another crowd-puller which links modern-day Alcester with its historic past.

The agricultural overtones of the fairs and markets have long ceased to exist, and although our modern sophisticated agricultural industry still plays an important role in the local economy, it is a far cry from the days when the town's very existence depended almost entirely on the successful exploitation of the land.

For centuries agriculture was generally based on one or more large open fields, subdivided into parallel 'ridge and furrow' strips. Alcester possessed one such field, situated on the southern and western side of the town, which was for the use of those living in the town itself. There were two further fields within the northern part of the manor, and these were for the use of the villagers of King's Coughton.

The various strips were allocated to the local peasant farmers and others, who worked them either singly or in blocks. In addition, there were also areas of meadow and common grazing land.

Over the years, as more and more strips were grouped together in blocks, some of them being enclosed on a piecemeal basis, the system became increasingly complicated to operate, and the whole matter of land tenure was one of considerable confusion. The boundaries of the meadows and grazing land had also become blurred.

By 1771 the situation had deteriorated to such an extent, that it was necessary for Alcester to resort to an Act of Parliament to sort matters out

An ox being roasted at the traditional mop fair in 1912

At one time Alcester's many public houses largely depended on beer brewed at the town's local brewery. This photograph of Evesham Street early this century shows The Bell, which still exists, and The Rose and Crown which closed in the 1960s. Jutting into the background is The Globe, demolished in the 1960s to make way for a new traffic island

once and for all. The result was the Alcester Enclosure Award which, if it did not please everyone, at least put local agriculture on the path to a more businesslike and manageable operation.

The Award documents, which are still in existence in the County Record Office in Warwick, clearly set out such details as the ownership of the land in all its categories, grazing rights, public and private rights of way, and even the use of certain areas of land for the extraction of materials for repairing the local roads.

The Award also set out regulations requiring each allotment of land to be enclosed by hedges, a system which still has its legacy in the boundary pattern of the countryside today, even if many of the original hedge-lines have since disappeared.

In many parts of the Midland counties, the old ridge and furrow system can still be discerned, although it is less apparent around Alcester than in some places. This is due to the fact that when Lord Hertford acquired the lordship of the manor in 1813, he had much of the farmland levelled, presumably to make it easier to work. The 'Dig for Victory' devotees of the Second World War also did their best to obliterate agricultural history, but even so the old pattern has not entirely disappeared. As one local writer eloquently puts it: 'Occasionally, when the sun is low or the snow is disappearing from the fields, the faint outline of the old ridge and furrow may still be seen.'

Following the 1771 Enclosure Award, Alcester's all-important farming activities settled down to a more orderly existence, which by the end of the following century had obviously made an impression on the Warwickshire Agricultural Society which chose the town on several occasions as the site of its annual show.

The actual show site was at Oversley Green, and contemporary newspaper accounts report the extraordinary enthusiasm with which the local people welcomed each show and its large influx of visitors. Alcester has always needed little excuse to indulge in colourful public celebrations – even up to the present day – and the Warwickshire Agricultural Society's Show was a splendid opportunity to deck the streets with bunting and to erect triumphal arches across the main road leading to the showground.

In those days Alcester possessed a railway station, and on show days special trains were provided to bring in the crowds of visitors from all over the county, and beyond. In a sense, these important county shows, which were also held at other locations apart from Alcester, helped to underline the vital

The Old Malthouse, a fine example of medieval timbering, as it appeared in about 1904

significance of the agricultural industry in Warwickshire, which is still widely recognised.

Nowadays, of course, the county is the home of the Royal Agricultural Society of England, based not many miles from Alcester, at the National Agricultural Centre at Stoneleigh, where the annual Royal Show is a massive undertaking of international status.

CHAPTER FIVE

Needles, Stage-coaches and Trains

Agriculture and the various trades and industries associated with it, may have dominated the life of the town for much of its history, but there was one other industry which, in its own way, had a no less significant impact on the local economy and the lives of the townsfolk. This was needlemaking, an industry indelibly associated with the valley of the River Arrow and places like Redditch and Studley, but not so often thought of in the context of the development of Alcester.

In fact, there was a time when the manufacture of needles was the town's greatest source of employment. In 1841, for instance, 174 people were recorded as needleworkers out of a total population of around 2,400. Ten years later, the number had risen to 274 – including children – although the town's population had remained fairly constant. During the nineteenth century, and until the industry died out in the present century, there were at least eighteen needle-manufacturing sites recorded in Alcester at one time or another, and there would almost certainly have been smaller back room workshops too, of which records no longer exist.

Needlemaking in the region seems to have started in the Studley area as early as the mid–1600s, soon spreading along the Arrow valley in both directions, to Redditch and to Alcester. The earliest evidence of anyone connected with the industry operating in Alcester, dates from the 1670s, and from that time onwards the production of needles became increasingly important in the town.

For a long period needlemaking was being operated on the basis of what today we would call a cottage industry, with the local people undertaking the individual, and often hazardous, processes in their own homes. There were straighteners, drillers, eyers, filers, grinders, scourers, pointers, polishers and many more, all contributing to the finished products.

By the eighteenth century it was realised that the existing water-mills, traditionally used for grinding corn, could also be harnessed to perform the scouring and pointing operations in needlemaking, and this not only boosted production, but relieved the outworkers of two of the processes most damaging to their health.

One such mill was Ragley Mill at the end of Ragley Mill Lane off the

The former Minerva needleworks in Station Road, a surviving monument to Victorian self-assurance. This impressive factory was built in 1880 by the Allwoods, one of Alcester's leading needlemaking families

Birmingham road, dating back to the thirteenth century and also known during its long life as both Alcester Mill and Priory Mill. Today, its milling days have long since passed and it survives as an attractive private residence. Another local mill, at King's Coughton, was actually built specifically as a needle mill towards the end of the eighteenth century, an indication of the growing importance of the industry at that time.

With the arrival of the Victorian era in the following century, needlemaking in Alcester was to undergo one more major change. With their customary ingenuity and flair for business, the Victorians realised that by introducing mechanised production methods, it was far more productive as well as economical, to gather together all the various needlemaking processes under one roof, rather than dispersing them among a large number of outworkers. The result was that several needle factories and smaller workshops were established in the town, and the old cottage industry began to diminish, although a limited amount of outwork persisted right into the present century.

Despite the upsurge in production which the new factories ensured, the latter years of Victoria's reign also witnessed the beginning of the industry's decline in Alcester, as needlemaking became increasingly centred on Redditch and Studley.

The last of Alcester's needlemaking firms occupied premises at the lower end of Malt Mill Lane and specialised in the production of needles for surgical use. It ceased operating as recently as the 1980s and the workshops have now been demolished. But there are still several buildings surviving in the town as reminders of an ancient industry which once played so vital a role in local life.

Pre-eminent among these is the former Minerva factory in Station Road, an impressive three-storey edifice of decorative brick with rows of arched windows, built in 1880. It was the creation of the Allwood family, one of the great names in Alcester's needlemaking history, who started business in

The Eagle Works in Bull's Head Yard, one of many needle factories which operated in Alcester over the years, ceased production soon after the First World War. This photograph was taken in 1978 shortly before the building was demolished

Henley Street, an important centre of the industry in earlier times. Sadly, the heyday of their new factory was short-lived. After a little more than thirty years the Allwood firm ceased trading, and the once proud Minerva works was auctioned off.

It has been the home of several industrial enterprises since then, and has seen the production of a variety of products, from springs and golf balls, to supermarket trolleys and metal substitutes for corset bones.

Among other surviving buildings dotted about the town, which were once associated with needlemaking, are the former workshops behind the handsome dwelling on the corner of Priory Road and School Road. They were occupied by one Joseph Harrison, whose firm not only produced needles for much of the last century, but later demonstrated its versatility by diversifying into the manufacture of pins and the special buckles needed to tighten the rigging wires on the early aircraft flown by the Royal Flying Corps in the First World War.

Yet another former needle factory occupied the building at the top of Malt Mill Lane, opposite the picturesque Old Malthouse. This was known as the Excelsior Works and housed the factory of Thomas Cooke in the second half of the last century, before being acquired by the grand-sounding Alcester Needlemakers' Society Limited. This latter organisation traded until 1936 when, with a keen eye on business opportunity, it changed its name to the Alcester Productive Society to reflect its growing involvement in the production of knitwear and other clothing. Unfortunately, the Board of Trade of the day did not particularly approve of the antiquated way the firm operated, and rather than change its ways, it closed down altogether. Today, although repainted and otherwise cosmetically improved, the building is little changed externally since those momentous days, and now serves as an attractive private residence.

Although, as we have seen, Alcester's needle industry eventually met with a gradual decline towards the end of the last century, at least some of those who were involved in it showed commendable entrepreneurial flair, by taking the precaution of changing their industrial course before it was too late.

Encouraged by the latest boom trade in Coventry, they embarked upon the manufacture of bicycles. Cycling was beginning to assume enormous popularity throughout the country, thanks largely to the invention of the so-called safety bicycle, which incorporated the very latest technical innovations – a chain-driven wheel and pneumatic tyres. Alcester played a significant if relatively brief role in this latest industrial success story.

Ragley Mill was one of the locations which became involved. The grinding of corn had, of course, occupied it for centuries, and it had made its mark on the local needle industry by eventually scouring virtually all the

The interior of Joseph Harrison's Abbey Works in Bleachfield Street in 1915. Starting as a needlemaker in Priory Road, he switched to bicycle manufacture, and then to the production of motor cycle side-cars seen here

needles produced in the town by the various manufacturers. Now, in the 1890s, its hard-working machinery was put to yet another use by the Patent Turned Spoke Company who adapted it to produce bicycle spokes.

Meanwhile, Joseph Harrison's versatile needleworks in Priory Road were already involved in the new industry and were producing their own bicycles. By 1903 the demand necessitated larger premises, and new workshops known as the Abbey Works were built in Bleachfield Street, capable of producing some sixty bicycles a week.

Unfortunately, bicycle production was obliged to cease during the First World War, when the factory turned its hand to the manufacture of side-cars for motor-cycles, giving them the same trade name of Speedwell as had been used for the bicycles. When the war ended, the firm branched out into more general woodwork, and another chapter in Alcester's industrial history had closed.

Until the latter half of the Victorian era, Alcester, like any other country town, had been largely self-sufficient. Most of its trades and industries relied on locally-produced raw materials, many of them, as we have seen, emanating from the land. A notable exception, of course, was the basic wire required for needlemaking, which was brought in from outside, but in the main the people of Alcester, and those living in the dependent villages and hamlets round about, relied on the town and its own resources for their livelihood.

But Alcester, like so many other places, was to witness a dramatic and rapid change in its lifestyle with the arrival of the railway. This new era for the town dawned in 1866, and with it came not only an unprecedented ease of communication with the rest of the country, but a gradual decline of many of the long-established trades and industries whose products could be brought in more easily and cheaply from Birmingham and the other large manufacturing centres.

For centuries, travel between Alcester and anywhere outside its immediate environs, had at best been difficult and at worst impossible. The situation improved to a limited extent during the eighteenth century, with the introduction of the turnpike system which, through Acts of Parliament, saw

One of Alcester's principal needlemaking families were the Dowdeswells whose factory was in Bleachfield Street. This was their work-force in about 1890

the setting up of special turnpike trusts responsible for specific stretches of road. Each trust was empowered to charge a toll to passing travellers, and the revenue they gained was used to repair and maintain the roads in question. The system, which certainly improved the reliability and timekeeping of stage-coaches, remained in operation until the 1880s, when the newly-inaugurated county councils took over the task of road maintenance.

Numerous turnpike trusts operated in and around Alcester, the first, in 1754, controlling the road through the town from Stratford to Bradley Green near Feckenham, and the road linking Alcester to Bromsgrove. In 1778, the Alcester to Evesham road was turnpiked, with an offshoot trust being formed a few years later to take over separate responsibility for the section between the town and the village of Norton.

The last of the local turnpikes was formed in 1814, and this linked the village of Wootton Wawen to Alcester's Gunnings Bridge, the ancient crossing-place on the River Arrow joining the town to the adjacent community of Oversley.

Although today Oversley is, to all intents and purposes, a part of Alcester, the amalgamation of the two places is of fairly recent origin in terms of their long histories. It was in 1909 that Alcester's parish boundary was extended to include Oversley, and in the 1950s the civil boundary was similarly extended.

When responsibility for Gunnings Bridge was assumed by the new county council towards the end of the last century, there must have been a considerable feeling of relief in Alcester, as this ancient river-crossing had reached an advanced state of deterioration on more than one occasion in the past.

Early in the seventeenth century, for instance, when it was presumably of wooden construction, it was reported as being 'in great decay', and that the Lord of the Manor, Lord Brooke, was considering the construction of 'a good stone bridge, out of his good and charitable disposition'.

His Lordship's goodness and charity were evidently lacking on this occasion, as he was fined a few years later for not having undertaken any repairs to the bridge at all.

The old bridge continued to cause problems over the ensuing years, and in 1839 it was described as 'dangerous' by the turnpike trust responsible for the road linking it to Wootton Wawen. Once again the Lord of the Manor became involved – this time Lord Hertford – and the trust undertook to ensure the bridge was safe enough to support coach traffic if his lordship would pay the required sum for repair work. The outcome of the proposal is not recorded, but the old bridge was eventually replaced by the stone-dressed brick structure which still spans the Arrow today.

The old turnpike trusts operated a series of toll-houses and toll-gates in

The toll-house at Arrow with its toll-gate across the road to Evesham, *c.* 1860. The old building still stands as a private house

order to collect their dues from the travelling public. Although the gates have, of course, long disappeared, one or two of the original toll-houses still survive as unmistakable reminders of a significant chapter in the story of local road transport. One of these can be seen on the outskirts of the town at Arrow, where the Worcester road branches off the main road from Alcester to Evesham. Another still looks out over the Stratford to Alcester road, at the junction of the lane to the village of Haselor.

By the end of the second decade of the last century, the various toll roads were providing reasonable links with the neighbouring towns, and Alcester's days of relative remoteness were finally at an end. For a time, following the turnpiking of local roads, the town was designated as a stopping-place on the main stage-coach route linking London and Holyhead via Shrewsbury, but this brief period of transport glory did not last long. When the great Scottish engineer Thomas Telford transformed the old Roman road of Watling Street into the major trunk route we now call the A5, the Holyhead coaches used this rather than the less direct route through Alcester.

But despite this loss to the town, the local stage-coach traffic increased dramatically for a time. There were regular services operated by coaches bearing such splendid names as Britannia, Shamrock, Quicksilver and Pilot, to destinations as far away as London, Aylesbury, Gloucester, Bristol and Leicester, as well as to nearer places like Birmingham and Kidderminster. Later, as the long-distance services began to decline, there was more emphasis on local routes to Evesham, Worcester, Stratford, Warwick, Leamington, and still of course to Birmingham.

This was the heyday of the town's coaching inns, which provided welcoming stopping-places for weary travellers as they passed through the town, or for whom Alcester was the final terminus. At first, the principal coaching inn was The Swan, which still graces the corner of Swan Street and Bleachfield Street, but after a few years the coaches were stopping at other inns too. Two of these, like The Swan, still exist as public houses – The Bear in the High Street and The White Lion in Evesham Street – but The Angel in Church Street has long since closed, although the elegant building still survives, while The Globe, as we have seen earlier, was demolished in the 1960s. Happily, no such fate has overtaken the nearby Cross Keys on the Stratford Road, a delightful little pub which has been in business since the 1860s, although never as a coaching inn, occupying what was originally a pair of cottages.

Swan Street in 1914, showing two of Alcester's principal coaching inns, The Swan in the left foreground, which is still here, and The Globe in the background, demolished in the 1960s

The High Street, *c.* 1960. The low gabled building in the centre is The Bear Hotel, once an important coaching inn

As the nineteenth century progressed and the new railway network spread its tentacles ever more widely, so the old stage-coaches ceased to operate. By 1866, when Alcester became a railway town, the coach services had ceased altogether, although the very latest horse-buses were now providing a number of local services. These, in turn, gave way to motor buses, and by the early 1920s, the town could boast regular if infrequent services to Birmingham, Redditch, Bromsgrove, Evesham, Worcester and Stratford.

The arrival of the railway had a profound effect not only on public transport but on the life of the town generally. With its new railway station, Alcester was now effectively linked to virtually the whole of Britain, and things would never be quite the same again.

The first line to serve the town was a somewhat meandering loop off the main Birmingham to Gloucester line, which it left at Barnt Green and rejoined at Ashchurch near Tewkesbury. The route not only included the burgeoning town of Redditch, but also served the main market garden centres of the Vale of Evesham. It was operated initially by the Evesham and

'The Unicorn', an early horse-bus which would have been a familiar sight on Alcester's streets around the turn of the century

Redditch Railway Company, which later became part of the Midland Railway and then the LMS, before finally being absorbed by British Railways with the advent of nationalisation in 1948.

When Alcester's station was first built in 1866, only the southern section of the line to Ashchurch had been completed. Two years later the route was extended northwards and the town's railway era began in earnest.

In 1876 an entirely new line was built to join up with the existing one a short distance to the north of the town. This was the Alcester Railway which ran through Great Alne to the Stratford-upon-Avon Railway Company's line at Bearley, eventually to become part of the giant GWR network.

The fortunes of the Alcester Railway were decidedly mixed. During the First World War it was closed and the rails were lifted for transportation across the Channel where they were to be re-laid for military purposes. Unfortunately, they never arrived at their destination, and if contemporary

Midland Red buses line up in the High Street in September 1928 ready to depart for a children's outing

accounts can be relied upon, they now lie rusting beneath the sea following the sinking of the ship which was carrying them.

But this was not yet to be the end of the ill-fated line. It was re-laid in 1923 and operated until the outbreak of the Second World War when its passenger services were once more suspended. It was, however, briefly reopened to provide transport for war workers travelling between Coventry and a factory at Great Alne, and was used for occasional goods trains until its final demise in the 1950s.

Those who can remember the old line, do so with affection, and still refer to the GWR tank engine which plied to and fro through the Warwickshire countryside as 'The Coffee Pot', on account of the prominent brass dome which characterised the shape of its boiler.

Alcester's other line lasted almost to the end of the steam era, losing its passenger services in 1962 and freight traffic two years later. Nowadays, the old station building survives as a private dwelling, its 'Station House' name-plate appropriately embellished with a picture of an early steam locomotive. But little evidence of the line itself remains, much of its former course having been reclaimed by nature or buried beneath modern housing developments.

Another almost ironic act of finality had been the demolition in 1960 of the former Railway Inn round the corner from the station in Birmingham Road. Although its days as licensed premises had, in fact, ended as long ago as the 1920s, it had nevertheless stood as a symbolic reminder of its railway associations which dated back to the 1870s.

Even for those who can still remember Alcester's railway heyday, it is difficult to realise now that the area around the site of the former station was once the station yard, with sidings busily handling such commodities as coal and timber, as well as cattle bound for the local abattoir.

By the 1960s the all-pervading motor car was increasingly making its mark, and Alcester's railway history had finally succumbed to its untimely but inevitable end.

A branch line train from Bearley arrives at Alcester station in 1910 hauled by the GWR tank engine affectionately known as 'The Coffee Pot'

CHAPTER SIX

Schools, Schooling and the Three Rs

Alcester may have suffered ignominious banishment from the railway map of Britain, a fact which many would maintain has left the town poorer as a result, but in the field of education it can count itself a good deal more fortunate.

For its relatively modest size, the town is remarkably well served by schools, with no less than six flourishing establishments looking after the educational needs, not only of the youngsters within the town itself, but of the many who come in from outlying areas.

But the schools of today – three catering for infants and juniors, and three for the pupils of secondary school age – are, in fact, the legacy of a chequered history which has reflected the changing attitudes to education over many years.

Alcester Grammar School, as we have seen, started off life as a chantry school at a time when the limited educational opportunities which were available were vested in the church, and it fortuitously escaped closure when so many chantries and other religious establishments were dissolved in the sixteenth century. Boosted in 1598 by an endowment of £20 a year in the will of Alcester's far-sighted benefactor, Walter Newport, it continued to serve the locality over the centuries in its old stone building in the lane known as Birch Abbey in the southern part of the town.

Although described for much of its early life as Newport's Free School, this historic place of learning did eventually find itself obliged to admit fee-paying boys, some of whom were accepted as boarders. As a result, by the last century, the word 'Free' in the school's title began to give way to the term 'Grammar'.

By modern standards, the school was never a large one, and until Victorian times, education was largely considered the privilege of the well-to-do and an unnecessary interference in the more important matter of a child's ability to perform manual work.

Even in the early years of the present century, when other schools existed in Alcester and there was a more enlightened approach to education, a local directory reported that 'the Grammar School' had a total attendance of only forty-two day boys, and just four boarders. Three of the day boys were evidently being educated free.

The old Newport's Free School building in Birch Abbey, photographed in 1903 when it was more commonly known as the Grammar School

These relatively low numbers may have been partly due to the limited accommodation in the old Birch Abbey premises, for in 1912 the new grammar school was opened by the side of the Birmingham road, the starting age was reduced to six, and the number of pupils – by now including girls as well – had soon reached 150. It continued as a fee-paying establishment until the Education Act of 1944, and today, under the aegis of Warwickshire County Council, it caters for more than 570 boys and girls from Alcester and the surrounding area.

With such a long history, it is not surprising to find that the administration of the school was beset by the occasional problem over the years. One such episode occurred in the 1880s when the headmaster of the day was widely criticised for his apparent inability to manage the school satisfactorily. He was not only described as 'unqualified', but the poor fellow was also deaf and myopic. As a result, a group of local businessmen, together with the High and Low Bailiff, brought in a teacher from Redditch in order to set up a rival establishment.

The fact that this new school was launched is confirmed by entries in local directories for the years up to 1888, which refer to the 'day and boarding' facilities of the new 'Alcester Commercial School' in Church Street. What happened to it after that is not clear, although its disappearance from the scene could well have had something to do with the fact the unpopular headmaster at the Grammar School – the man who had allegedly caused all the problems in the first place – had retired in 1887. Unfortunately, his successor, a cleric, seems to have been equally lacking in competence, and although contemporary reports pointedly speak of his laziness, he managed to prolong his incumbency until 1893, when he was replaced by an altogether more suitable headmaster who quickly started to restore the school's ailing reputation.

The suitability of headmasters apart, the pupils themselves appear to have endured a spartan existence, which in our modern age of children's rights would provoke an instant outcry. Records from around the middle of the last century, for instance, state that the school day was timed to start at seven o'clock, to enable boarders to work for one hour before breakfast. It is a matter of conjecture as to how they would have coped with the assimilation of knowledge at that early hour, particularly during periods when increased numbers meant that the unfortunate lads were obliged to sleep two to a bed in their attic dormitories.

Apart from the old Grammar School, Alcester also had its so-called National School, an establishment for both boys and girls, set up in 1843 in

The original National School in School Road which has now given way to a development of retirement homes

association with the grand-sounding National Society for the Education of the Poor in the Principles of the Established Church.

This school, under the direction of the church and supported by voluntary contributions, was built in what is today known as School Road. Despite the fact that it was supposed to cater for the poorer of Alcester's children, the pupils were nevertheless expected to pay a modest levy, amounting to a few coppers a week, until fees for this type of school were abolished by the government in 1891.

In 1872 the school was enlarged and improved, a timely measure intended to forestall any attempt under the Education Act of 1870, to set up in Alcester one of the non-denominational Board Schools which were intended to serve areas where the standard of exisiting elementary education was thought to be lacking

The ploy was evidently successful, for the efficiency of the National School was not challenged, and within a few years it was even considered opportune to open an additional department for infants.

Soon after the turn of the century, another new school was opened in the town, this time for the Roman Catholics. Since 1889 they had worshipped in their new church in Priory Road, and used it also for educational purposes until separate school premises next door had been completed in 1902. These served their original purpose until well into the 1960s, although even today the old Edwardian building continues to provide a much valued service by accommodating a play-school for toddlers.

Yet another chapter in the story of Alcester's schools is provided by an unusual establishment in Priory Road which started off life as a non-conformist Sunday school, but which, in 1911, became a centre for craftwork used at various times by children from a number of local schools. It lasted until the early 1950s, when its equipment was moved to a new department at the Grammar School, and the building has since served as a private dwelling.

Alcester's schooling scene today is a far cry from the visions of Walter Newport, and indeed from the basic education system pioneered by the Victorians. Apart from the historic grammar school, there are now two other establishments providing secondary education – the former Greville High School of the 1960s, which became Alcester High School in 1985, and the Roman Catholic St Benedict's. The building once occupied by the old National School in School Road has now disappeared in favour of retirement homes, replaced by a separate infants' school nearby, and a modern Church of England junior school. The latter, in St Faith's Road, neighbours its Roman Catholic counterpart, which also caters for infants.

All the Alcester schools so far mentioned now come under the jurisdiction of the local education authority, regardless of their individual origins. But

The High Street as it was in the latter years of the last century. Premises at No. 21 (approximately next to the parked wagons) accommodated Franklin's Day and Boarding School for more than thirty years

there is one other component in the story of the town's schools, which, although now confined to the pages of history, once played a colourful and occasionally eccentric role in Alcester's day-to-day life.

This was the extraordinary assortment of privately-run establishments which existed from the latter years of the eighteenth century until well into the present century. In number and variety, they were at their peak during Victoria's reign, and many were founded at a time when it was possible for anyone, whatever their qualifications – even if they possessed none at all – to start a school. Some of the establishments were no doubt run by opportunists intent upon making a quick profit from hard-pressed mothers who were themselves earning a meagre daily living in one of the town's needle workshops.

Well over twenty privately-run schools existed in the town at one time or another, and by all accounts at least some of them were perfectly respectable, offering a reasonable education to their pupils. Poplar Cottage School in Evesham Street seems to have been one of the more reputable establishments, operating for much of the last century. Described as a 'ladies' boarding

From about 1874 until the early years of the present century, Churchill House (on the extreme left) was occupied by an exclusive 'Home School for Young Ladies' founded by Miss Mary Roseanna Steward

school', it issued a prospectus assuring parents that their children would be 'liberally boarded and carefully instructed in the usual branches of a polite and useful education'. It was stressed, too, that the pupils would have 'particular attention paid to their morals, health and comfort'.

The 'polite and useful education' evidently embraced reading, writing, arithmetic, English grammar, geography, history and needlework, all of which, including full board, cost 20 guineas a year. French, music, dancing and drawing were listed as 'extras', and so was 'washing' which presumably referred to the pupils' garments rather than their personal ablutions.

Another Victorian school which lasted for more than a few years was Franklin's Day and Boarding School which operated from premises at No. 21 High Street. Unusually, this particular establishment was coeducational. Exclusively for 'young ladies', however, was the school run by the redoubtable Miss Mary Roseanna Steward, first in Evesham Street, and then in Churchill House, the elegant villa bearing the date 1688 which still graces Henley Street by the side of the Town Hall.

On the other side of the road, yet another Victorian school operated in the attractive timbered house, now partly a shop, which rather engagingly stands at right-angles to the adjacent Baptist Chapel and the other buildings in the street. Described as both a boarding and day school, it was run by one Sarah Mascall and her daughter, another Sarah, the latter eventually assuming sole responsibility. Teaching, of course, was considered a perfectly respectable occupation for unmarried ladies, and in the case of the young Sarah, her school lasted for something like a quarter of a century, before the building changed its use to that of a bakery.

If private schools for girls were fairly numerous, their male counterparts also figure in contemporary records. In the early years of the last century, for instance, an establishment known as Johnson's Boarding School for Young Gentlemen seems to have been operating in the High Street, later moving to premises in Henley Street. It obviously made its mark, for after a few years it was being referred to by the far grander title of Academy. Even so, like so many other schools of that period, it was a relatively short-lived enterprise, and by the middle of the century it had ceased to be recorded in the census returns and had presumably closed.

At the other end of the educational scale was a school for infants being run in the early 1850s from a cottage in Gas House Lane. The teacher was the 76-year-old owner of the cottage, Hannah Lea, whose venture, perhaps not surprisingly, is another which does not appear to have lasted very long.

The last century was certainly a colourful period in Alcester's educational history. Schools of varying degrees of competency came and went like mushrooms in a summer meadow, often catering for no more than a handful of pupils in the parlour of a private dwelling. Others were run on more professional lines, and were respected as worthy places of education. But whatever their status, they were, with few exceptions, run by a splendid succession of Dickensian characters, not a few of whom seem to have been formidable and eccentric spinsters. Now they have all long gone, but in their day they undoubtedly made their mark on the eventful history of Alcester's schools and schooling.

CHAPTER SEVEN

Architectural Heritage and a Taste for Cakes

Visually, few would disagree that Alcester is one of the Midland region's most attractive towns, still unspoilt by such phenomena as the high-rise blocks of flats and multi-storey car parks which have so often disfigured other places in recent years. The town has certainly not entirely escaped examples of insensitive planning decisions, but on the whole it has reached the late twentieth century with much of its intrinsic charm and character intact.

The principal reason for this is the wealth of older buildings, some admittedly hiding their true age behind later cosmetic façades, which have survived to contribute to Alcester's rich architectural heritage. Almost without exception, if one delves into their historical background, many fascinating pictures emerge of the life and times of Alcester and its people over the centuries.

But there have been some notable architectural losses too, and even if the demolition of such buildings was convincingly – or unconvincingly – justified at the time, their disappearance, in most cases, has undoubtedly left the town a little poorer in visual if not in economic terms.

One such building stood at the junction of Gas House Lane and Stratford Road until it was pulled down in the 1950s. It was a substantial house of timbering and rendered brick, dating in all probability from the sixteenth century, and known for much of its life as The Great House or The Old House. From the late 1700s until 1834 it had served as Alcester's workhouse for the poor, but by the time it was demolished it had been subdivided into tenements to such an extent, that it had earned itself the affectionate sobriquet of The Rookery.

Old photographs show the building as an impressive example of the timbered architecture of its time, even if in its final days a few judicious repairs would not have gone amiss. Its controversial demolition, and the outcry it provoked, did have one beneficial result. It led to the formation of the Alcester Civic Society which has since maintained an eagle eye on local planning decisions and their possible implications on the town's architectural heritage.

Known as The Rookery, this sixteenth-century timbered building on Stratford Road was demolished in the late 1950s. It had formerly served as Alcester's workhouse

The Rookery in the course of demolition, an act which resulted in the formation of the Alcester Civic Society

Early Victorian Oversley House, now converted into homes for the elderly, was originally built as a workhouse to replace its overcrowded predecessor on Stratford Road

The Rookery was replaced by a not unattractive block of mews-type dwellings which perpetuate the old name, and they are certainly a far cry from their predecessor's earlier role as a workhouse. The inmates who once lodged in the old building were transferred in 1836 to a new workhouse just beyond Gunnings Bridge. This purpose-built replacement still survives to this day as Oversley House, although now skilfully converted into apartments for the elderly. Its residents are no doubt reassured to know that the former workhouse infirmary, now converted into Alcester Hospital, is conveniently close by.

The town's workhouse was one tangible reflection of local concern for the poor and underprivileged, who were evidently so numerous in 1871, that in just one period of seven weeks they were given well over 2,000 quarts of soup.

The problem of caring for these unfortunate people had been around for a long time, and as early as the 1650s, a quarter sessions report stated that 'Alcester is a town overburdened with poor'.

One way of dealing with the situation was to set up charities to provide such facilities as apprenticeships for the young and almshouses for the elderly, and the seventeenth century saw several such remedies being introduced. In 1659, for instance, four almshouses were built in what is now Birmingham

Part of the fine timbered building in Swan Street known as Hodge's Bakery, as it appeared in the 1930s. This building was pulled down in the 1950s

Road, and these survived until the 1950s. Another four were sited in Bleachfield Street in 1680, to end in demolition in the late 1960s. Even as recently as the turn of the present century, a row of six almshouses was built by the side of the Birmingham Road for the benefit of deserving local tradesmen or their widows, and these still exist to this day.

Less fortunate than these last-named almshouses was an old timber-framed house, reputed to have been one of the finest in Alcester, which was pulled down in the 1950s. This was known as Hodge's Bakery and once stood at the junction of Swan Street and Evesham Street opposite the 230-year-old Globe Inn which itself succumbed to the bulldozers in 1965 as we have seen in an earlier chapter. The shop which has replaced the old bakery may be functionally more convenient, but it demonstrably lacks the picture-book charm of its ill-fated predecessor.

This part of the town has seen more changes than most, for The Globe's demolition was to provide a site for the present traffic roundabout, overlooked by a typically utilitarian brick complex of the 1960s, comprising a health clinic, library, police station, magistrates' courts and fire station. This development may look somewhat incongruous architecturally, but it is not out of scale with its surroundings and its component parts provide valuable public services.

But to dwell unduly on what Alcester has lost and on what has appeared in its place, denies recognition of the many town-centre scenes where change, if it has occurred at all, has been far less dramatic. Alcester's architecture embraces every period from medieval to the present day, and there is a surprisingly large number of timber-framed buildings surviving from the sixteenth and seventeenth centuries. In many cases these are now camouflaged behind brick façades, a trend which became popular in the eighteenth and nineteenth centuries when the abundance of local clay was being increasingly used by an expanding brick-making industry. In other cases, older timber-framed buildings were converted in their entirety into brick dwellings, although their original form of construction can often still be discerned.

One notable group of medieval timbered buildings which have survived the centuries more or less in their original form, are those gracing the northern end of Malt Mill Lane. They were impeccably restored in the 1970s, and as a result they deservedly earned a Civic Trust Award.

The High Street also contains several fine examples of timber-framed buildings, some still appearing virtually unchanged since they were constructed, others encased within later shells. The street itself, in terms of its

The 230-year-old Globe Hotel was demolished in the 1960s to make way for a new traffic roundabout

The High Street, *c.* 1919. The large building on the right, now occupied by the local Unionist Club, stands on the site of the old Bull Ring and effectively narrows the street at its southern end

shape and layout, has remained almost unaltered since medieval times, or even earlier, although many of the buildings bordering it have inevitably seen change. It is thus one of the most interesting thoroughfares in the town, and well repays the inquisitive observer who is able to unravel its historical secrets.

It has been known as the High Street for no more than a couple of centuries, and was originally described by various names alluding to the uses to which it was put. The lower end, near its junction with Stratford Road, was known as the Bull Ring, the area where unfortunate cattle were cruelly baited. Since the middle of the eighteenth century, the building now occupied by the town's Unionist Club has occupied the major part of this infamous site, jutting into the street's southernmost section which it partly encloses.

The centre section of the street was called the Sheepmarket, or Beastmarket, and there are records of animals being sold here as late as the second half of the nineteenth century. The northern part of the street was The Shambles, where the town's many butchers once killed and sold their meat, and the name of the narrow alley-way leading off it – Bull's Head Yard – still evokes a picture of those early days.

This northern part of the High Street contains some fine examples of

In the 1950s the High Street building still occupied today by Bunting's the grocers briefly revealed its basic timber construction during restoration work

timber-framed architecture, both visible and hidden. Bunting's grocery store on the street's western side is a case in point, and its smart rendered frontage masks the original timbering which was briefly revealed in the 1950s when the building was being repaired. Many old timbers also survive inside, providing a delightful if somewhat incongruous setting for the displays of twentieth-century groceries.

The splendid representation of a sugar loaf – the traditional trade sign of the grocer – which is suspended above the shop's entrance, was rehung in 1955, when it had probably already been in existence for a very long time. Original deeds indicate that as early as the seventeenth century the property was in use as a chandlery business, becoming a grocers in the following century, a role it has maintained right up to the present day. In fact, the shop can boast an impressive record of retail service to the public spanning no less than 300 years.

The building next door is another notable example of the High Street's wealth of timber-framing, even if its pretty bow-windowed frontage now conceals the fact. At the rear, however, its original Tudor timber construction is here for all to see, as this part of the building, which is reached down yet another of the High Street's ancient alleys, or tueries, now serves as The Tudor Rose Tea Rooms. This name, incidentally, alludes to the Tudor rose motif decorating the tea room's fine moulded ceiling, which was discovered some years ago when a layer of later plaster was removed.

On the opposite side of the road, the name of an erstwhile inn retained by the Turk's Head craft gallery, is a reminder of the fact that Alcester once boasted an extraordinarily large number of hostelries. The Turk's Head's long history as an inn ended in 1978, by which time its previous names of The Buck and Breeches and then The Bush had long been forgotten. At one time it was one of seven inns in the High Street, a number which has now dwindled to three – The Bear, The Royal Oak, and The Three Tuns, an establishment which, after closing as an inn in 1900 and then serving at various times as a shop and restaurant, has now once again reverted to its former function.

Just along the road from The Three Tuns is a row of four modern shops – somewhat obtrusive in architectural terms – which stand on a site once occupied by Alcester's grandiose Corn Exchange and an old cottage. The Corn Exchange was built in 1857, and for a couple of decades or so it performed its intended role as a centre for the purchase and sale of cereals and other crops. But the need for its services began to diminish, and it became increasingly used as a social centre and meeting place, offering such attractions as theatrical performances, concerts and the 'penny readings' so loved by the Victorians.

Contemporary records of the widely varying entertainments offered at the Corn Exchange reveal such delights as performances by 'Miss Duncan's Dramatic Company', an 'Enchanted Palace of Illusions' presented by someone calling himself Signor Bosco, and an unspecified 'rope feat' performed by the Davenport Brothers. The building flourished in its new guise until 1924 when it succumbed to the demands of the new cinema age by becoming first the Alcester Picture House and then the Regent. As such, it lasted until 1965, when it was finally beaten by the magnetic attraction of television and was demolished.

Although, in its day, the old Corn Exchange served many a useful purpose, the architectural purists considered it an affront to the overall appearance of the High Street. Stone-built in the flamboyant Italianate style, with prominent pilasters topped by a large stone sheaf of corn, it stood out self-consciously among its smaller scale neighbours. Ironically, the critics who condemned the

A 1904 view of the High Street showing the now demolished Corn Exchange dominating the right hand side

style of its architecture and applauded its demise, have been similarly unimpressed by the appearance of the shops which replaced it.

With the disappearance of the Corn Exchange, the High Street was left with only one stone-faced building, the aptly-named Stone House next to The Royal Oak. This diminutive cottage has had a chequered existence, serving at various times as an inn called The Three Horseshoes, a coffee house, and as a Victorian workingmen's club.

One can only speculate as to how the building fared in its last-named role. Owned at the time by the Lord of the Manor, it was given by him to the town so that it could be converted into a place in which the local working men could meet, away from the 'evil influences' of the many public houses. The facilities included a reading room and various other innocuous 'amusements', not exactly the sort of diversions capable of luring working men away from the ale houses with which they were all too familiar. Presumably though, it did succeed in attracting a clientele, even if it was somewhat limited.

The building's present next door neighbour is the modern post office of 1963, which replaced four timber-framed cottages. Its predecessor was accommodated in one of the handsome Georgian houses which grace Church Street, still recognised by older inhabitants as the Old Post Office. For much of the last century the building served as a bakery, even after it assumed its post office role, and it was by no means the only one in the town. In fact, bakery businesses were once so numerous in Alcester, that the place became known as Caketown, attracting customers from a wide surrounding area. At one time or another, no less than thirteen shops in the High Street were run by bakers, not to mention many more in other streets, a large number of them operating concurrently.

Just along the road from the Old Post Office building is another of Alcester's many former inns. This one was The Angel, and although it ceased to function as such as long ago as 1865 and now comprises private dwellings, its general appearance has not changed out of all recognition. The wide central gateway still exists as a reminder of the days when the stage-coaches trundled through to the yard at the rear, for horses to be changed and passengers refreshed.

There was an earlier Angel inn on the same site which was replaced when the present building and its immediate neighbours were built in Georgian times. Today, this whole row adds a delightful touch of Georgian distinction to Church Street, in the same way that the Lord Nelson inn recalls the same elegant era in Priory Road on the other side of the town.

The Lord Nelson is, in fact, not only notable for the elegance of its architecture, but for a curious detail on its colourful inn sign. The sign depicts the great one-eyed admiral with both his eyes intact.

The High Street, looking north, in 1949. At one time bakeries were so numerous in the town – there were thirteen in this street alone – that Alcester was widely known as Caketown

CHAPTER EIGHT

Past, Present, and Something to Celebrate

The area around the parish church would, of course, have looked very different in the days when the churchyard was virtually surrounded by shops and houses. These, as we have already seen, were collectively known as Shop Row and would have tended to give the churchyard the appearance of a hidden enclave rather than the broad and open aspect it enjoys today.

Only the western side of the churchyard is still bordered by buildings, the delightful cottages of narrow Butter Street, one of Alcester's most picturesque thoroughfares. Guarding its access from the High Street is the handsome red-brick former rectory of 1796, standing on the site of an even grander residence for the incumbent priest. Nowadays, in an age when church economics dictate a thriftier attitude towards the ownership of property, Alcester's rector lives in a more manageable house on a modern development to the north of the town.

The name of Butter Street harks back to the days when the sellers of dairy produce, notably butter, used the street to display and sell their wares. It was a sensible arrangement, as the street's narrow confines afforded protection from the sun, and provided a cooler environment than that of the adjacent Market Place.

The old Market Hall which, as we saw earlier, continues to serve Alcester as the Town Hall, marks the point where Church Street becomes Henley Street, another ancient thoroughfare endowed with considerable historic interest.

At its Town Hall end, the street can boast one of Alcester's most elegant buildings, pedimented and balconied Churchill House, which bears the date 1688. In fact, the date refers to the frontage only, as the house itself is considerably older than the reign of James II, and is essentially of timbered construction behind its ornate Jacobean façade. This, of course, was the house mentioned earlier which, as an establishment for the education of 'young ladies' during the latter years of the last century, was one of the many private schools exsisting in Alcester at that time.

The initials T & E L engraved on the downpipes provide a clue to the

Narrow Butter Street, site of the former butter market, one of Alcester's most attractive thoroughfares. This photograph dates from the 1940s

family responsible for transforming the house from a fairly ordinary timber building into one which, for its new-found elegance, would have raised more than a few seventeenth-century eyebrows. It was a Thomas Lucas who carried out the embellishment to his family home, and he endearingly included reference to his wife Elinor in the commemorative initials.

Next door to Churchill House is another of the inns which at one time were so common in Alcester. This is The Holly Bush, its name a twentieth-century addition, although the building itself is of considerable age.

The Holly Bush is still in business, but within a few paces are yet two more inns which are no longer trading as such. The first was originally known as The Greyhound's Head and then The Greyhound, and the building is a fine example of jettied timbering dating from the sixteenth century. It served its last ale in 1907 when its career as an inn was terminated due to the alleged 'unsanitary' conditions under which it had been operating.

The other former inn in this section of Henley Street is The Red Horse, built in the eighteenth century to replace an earlier timbered inn on the same site. It managed to keep trading until the late 1970s, but its memory lingers on in its name which now adorns the building in its present existence as a private dwelling. Another memory of its thirst-quenching days is provided by the engraved frosted glass of the front door. Teasingly it still proclaims the word Bar.

No. 19 Henley Street, reputed to be Alcester's oldest domestic building. Its cruck construction coupled with scientific tests indicate its year of origin as 1385

Arguably, if one discounts the historic Town Hall which dominates the southern end of Henley Street, the most interesting building hereabouts is the cottage numbered 19. Although from its outside appearance it would seem to date from the seventeenth century, it was discovered to be of cruck construction, embodying massive tree trunks as the basis of its timber framing. With the strength of this architectural evidence, No. 19 Henley Street is authoritatively considered to be the oldest domestic building in the town, with its origins going back to the fourteenth century. It therefore outdates other contenders for the title, the most notable of which is the magnificent timbered Old Malthouse on the corner of Church Street and Malt Mill Lane, which is no older than the early sixteenth century.

The ancient Henley Street building once had as its neighbour yet another of Alcester's multifarious pubs. This one was The Baker's Arms, so named because one of its Victorian landlords also ran a bakery business nearby. He was clearly an astute believer in the value of a little subtle advertising. Why else would he have named the pub after his bakery? The business ceased trading in the 1920s, and was eventually demolished in 1963 to make way for a new residential development.

Opposite the site of this erstwhile inn is an impressive red-brick Victorian building standing back from the road and still retaining something of the air of authority it once knew as Alcester's police station.

Built in about 1850, a few years before Alcester and then the whole county received its first professional police force, the building offered commodious accommodation for the town's law enforcers. Previous to this, as we have seen earlier, the town was policed by constables appointed by the Court Leet and later by the parish, and any malefactor whose crime deserved a spell in custody, was either put in the stocks or incarcerated in the lock-up which occupied a cramped space at one end of the Town Hall. Compared with this old lock-up, commonly known as 'The Hole', the relatively spacious cell accommodation in the new police station would have seemed positively luxurious to the town's wrongdoers.

The Town Hall in the traffic-free 1950s. Until the middle of the last century, local wrongdoers were incarcerated in the lock-up, which occupied a corner of the Town Hall's ground floor

The Alcester Fire Brigade's two horse-drawn appliances turn out on parade for the coronation of George V in 1911

When the modern block of public buildings off Priory Road was constructed in the late 1960s, the present up-to-date police station was included as a replacement for the Victorian building in Henley Street. The latter is now put to good use on behalf of the elderly by the Abbeyfields Society.

Alcester Fire Brigade is also now based in part of the modern Priory Road complex, backed by the latest fire-fighting technology and operating as an integral part of the Warwickshire Fire and Rescue Service. It is all a far cry from the early days when the firemen were volunteers, and their pumps were hauled by horses.

On some occasions the horses first had to be rounded up and caught so that they could be harnessed to the appliances. Even then the essential business of fire-fighting was often not as reliable as it might have been due to the shortage, or sometimes the complete lack, of water. Even after Alcester had its own piped water supply in 1879 – one of the first Warwickshire towns to benefit from what was then a remarkable innovation – the mains were often empty overnight. When called out to deal with nocturnal fires, the firemen were obliged to remove their 'engine' to the nearest stream or river in order to pump water to the scene of the conflagration.

The origin of the local fire brigade is somewhat obscure, although records do point to the fact that it had already been in existence for some years by the the middle of the last century, when it had its headquarters in the Town Hall.

By the 1880s the firemen had acquired new premises in Gas House Lane, and it was while they were based here in 1900 that one of Alcester's most

The Alcester Fire Brigade with its Merryweather motor fire-engine, outside the Almonry Museum in Evesham in the early 1920s

spectacular fires took place. It involved the Alcester Co-operative Society's building in Seggs Lane, and so fierce was the blaze that at one time much of adjacent Evesham Street was in danger of going up in flames. On this occasion, even with the deployment of both their appliances, the Alcester firemen found the challenge too great, and help had to be summoned from Stratford and Studley. That the fire was eventually extinguished, even if it did cause damage amounting to some £10,000, says a lot for the ability of the firemen of those long-forgotten days, operating with equipment which, by modern standards, was pitifully unsophisticated.

From about 1850 onwards, one of the innovations which would have kept the firemen particularly vigilant was the introduction of a gas supply to the town. The newly-founded Alcester Gas Light and Coke Company produced its gas at a plant by the side of Colebrook Lane, a thoroughfare which soon took on the less glamorous name of Gas House Lane by which it is still known to this day.

The new company, at first operating with just one gasholder, gradually extended its supply of gas to an ever-increasing number of residential and industrial users. After a few years, a second gasholder was introduced to cope with the demand.

One of the company's first assignments was to provide the town with street lighting, a system which lasted until after the Second World War, when it was converted to electricity in 1946. Two years later, the company was absorbed by its larger counterpart in Redditch which supplied the town direct, and local gas production ceased.

The two prominent gasholders, which had become familiar if unloved local landmarks, were eventually demolished in 1955, and within a few years Alcester, like much of the rest of Britain, was receiving its supply from deep below the North Sea. If those pioneering Victorians who first brought gas to the town could even have dreamed of such a development, they would have surely placed it firmly in the realms of fantasy.

Alcester, for many generations, has been noted as a closely-knit town possessing a much-cherished spirit of community. This has traditionally

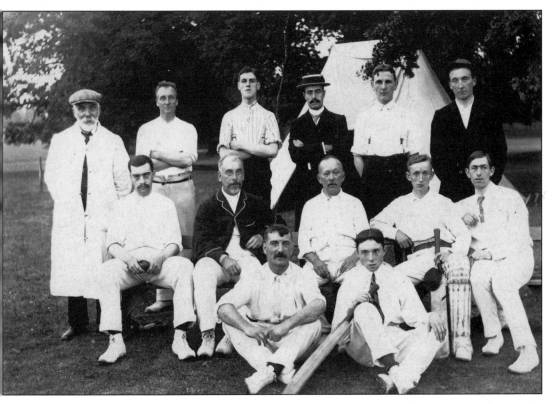

Alcester has long been noted for its sports clubs. These are the members of the Alcester and Ragley Cricket Club in 1910

manifested itself through a wide range of clubs and societies, and it is a situation as apparent today as it was a century or more ago. The various modern-day organisations may reflect different social attitudes from their earlier counterparts, but they have a no less dedicated following among Alcestrians.

Whereas at one time there were numerous societies concerned with moralistic, charitable and educational matters, the need for these is arguably less pressing today than was the case in the last century, and they have largely given way to different priorities and interests.

Charitable causes, of course, are still high on the agenda of the local branches of such worthy institutions as the Lions, Round Table and Rotary, the last-named possessing a special relationship with Alcester, as the town was chosen as the headquarters of Rotary International for Great Britain and Ireland.

The modern building occupied by this influential body is another which has played no small part in local history. It was originally built as offices for Alcester Rural District Council, but its role ceased when the council was abolished under the wide-ranging changes in local government which took place in 1974. Nowadays, in local authority terms, Alcester is governed by Stratford-upon-Avon.

The history of at least some of Alcester's clubs and societies can be traced

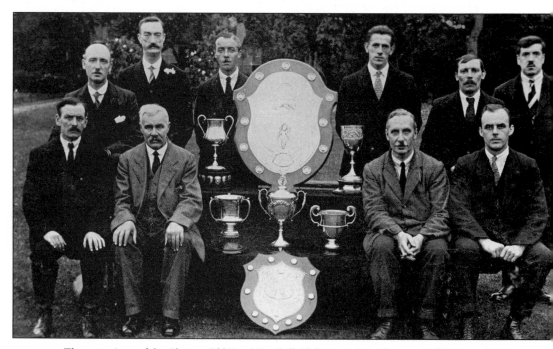

The committee of the Alcester Old Boys' Football Club were obviously proud of their trophies in the 1925/6 season.

back well into the last century or even earlier, and there are those concerned with sport, music and the arts in particular, which can look back further than most. The bowling enthusiasts, for instance, who play on a green at the end of Meeting Lane, are using hallowed turf which is said to have been the scene of bowls matches since Elizabethan times, although there is no firm documentary evidence to confirm such longevity. The ancient green continues to flourish, however, now in the possession of the Alcester Unionist Club.

Although a number of local clubs and societies enjoy their own facilities, many more make good use of the impressive-looking Greig Memorial Hall built in the late 1950s and joined more recently by a purpose-built indoor sports complex.

The hall was given to the town by one of its most distinguished businessmen, the founder of the David Greig grocery empire, in memory of his wife Hannah Susan. At one time, of course, the name David Greig was as familiar in high streets up and down the land as Sainsbury or Tesco is today, and the Greig Memorial Hall at Alcester is a fitting tribute to a beneficent local family.

The Greigs' home was at Upper Oversley Lodge, the grandiose castellated mansion which dominates its hilltop site between Alcester and the neighbouring village of Wixford. Popularly known for obvious reasons as Oversley Castle – not to be confused with Boteler's long-vanished castle of the twelfth century – it owes its origin to a visit paid by the Prince Regent to the second Marquess of Hertford at Ragley Hall, a mile or so away across the Arrow valley. The prince evidently suggested to Lord Hertford that the view from his home would be greatly enhanced by a castle on the distant hill. Such a suggestion from so eminent a visitor could hardly be ignored, and the elaborate folly was built.

There was a time in Alcester when the Friendly and Benefit Societies held sway among the townspeople, and during the last century in particular, they existed in large numbers. In those days, long before the welfare state gave its umbrella protection to the sick and deprived, such societies were not only needed but were vigorously supported. Some of those in Alcester were branches of national organisations, but a great many were purely local institutions, often based at the town's numerous inns.

In 1892, for example, no less than three-quarters of the population of the town belonged to one or other of these welfare organisations, whose many names ranged from the Old Bear Friendly Society and the Globe Sick and Dividend Society, to the United Patriots' Benefit Society, and the more down-to-earth Garden and Allotment Friendly Society.

By modern standards, the benefits received by the members of these

The parades of Alcester's numerous Friendly Societies were once a regular feature of local life. This parade of neatly-dressed members in Church Street took place in 1908

various bodies seem derisory, but in those days they represented an element of security which otherwise would have been absent from many people's lives. One society in the 1840s, for instance, charged a monthly subscription of 6*d* – 2½p in today's money – for which the member was entitled to 6*s* (30p) a week as sickness benefit, 2*s* (10p) a month after reaching the age of seventy, and the enormous sum of £5 for his dependants in the event of death.

These commendable societies were not only concerned with the welfare of their members. They were also the focus for a variety of social occasions, like their annual dinners and the regular parades they held in the streets which were guaranteed to bring out the crowds to line the pavements.

There were also other somewhat paternalistic bodies whose professed aim was to improve the morals and education of the so-called lower classes, by offering carefully monitored instruction and entertainment in an atmosphere of temperance and self-improvement. With as many as twenty inns in the

In 1911 Bleachfield Street was decked with its customary decorations to mark the coronation of George V

A makeshift balcony above a High Street shop provided a good vantage point for this group watching the 1911 coronation celebrations

The town band accompanies a church parade as it makes its way up the High Street to mark the coronation of George VI in 1937

town at the height of the Victorian era, each offering its own formidable temptations, the competition would seem to have been something of a problem.

Watching the parades of the local Friendly Societies was not the only diversion enjoyed by the local people. Any excuse to hold a street party and decorate the place with flags and bunting was eagerly grasped, as we saw earlier in the context of the Warwickshire Agricultural Society's visits to the town for its annual show.

Royal occasions and similar high spots in the national calendar have always been – and still are – celebrated with a fervour matched by few other towns anywhere. There are photographs in existence of many such occasions over the years, graphically reflecting Alcester's traditional ability to celebrate with unashamed enthusiasm.

The 1937 coronation provided an ideal opportunity for a typical Alcester street party. This one was held in Church Street outside the former post office

Bleachfield Street, considered at one time as not the most salubrious of thoroughfares, and definitely not the sort of place in which to venture alone, could nevertheless show the rest of the town a thing or two when it came to celebratory decorations. At no time were these more colourful than for the coronations of Edward VII and George V, when the two sides of the narrow street were linked by countless arches of patriotic decorations, and many of the buildings sported flags and pennants.

The High Street, too, has always put on a spectacular display, and even as recently as the wedding of the Prince and Princess of Wales, it was completely blocked by hundreds of revellers dancing beneath festoons of bunting.

The end of the Second World War gave Alcester another worthy excuse to

A proud member of the Church Lads' Brigade leads a parade of fellow members down the High Street shortly after the end of the Second World War

celebrate, even if it had been scarcely touched by the hostilities. Apart from a few stray bombs round about, the construction of some dummy decoy airfields in the surrounding countryside, and intrusive air-raid shelters which made their appearance in the High Street and Bleachfield Street, Alcester was spared the horrors inflicted upon other less fortunate Midland towns.

Good fortune has, in fact, played no small part in Alcester's long and fascinating story. That the town exists at all, at least in its present form, is because the Romans appreciated the strategic value of the river-crossing settlement they discovered here, and set about developing it. Over the ensuing centuries Alcester has taken in its stride the influences of each successive period of English history, and has been able to adapt accordingly. Even the slaughter and destruction of the English Civil Wars passed the town by with relatively little effect.

The social and economic pressures of the industrial revolution certainly made their mark, but only minimally compared with certain other Midland communities which, as a result, have expanded into unlovely industrial conurbations still bearing the scars which 'progress' inflicted on them.

Alcester's gentler era of leatherworking, needlemaking, and malting have all passed gracefully into the chapters of history, leaving behind a fascinating assortment of architectural legacies as reminders that they ever existed. Their place today is taken by the light industries of the twentieth century, almost entirely centred, with commendable unobtrusiveness, on a small development near the erstwhile railway station, and a larger industrial estate on the town's northern outskirts.

Each successive generation of Alcestrians has, no doubt, looked back on the days of its immediate predecessor and pointed to the varying causes and effects of change, both good and bad. This has been as inevitable in the past as it still is today. But the fact is that the town has survived into the latter years of the twentieth century with a countenance still fairer than most, and its character largely unsullied.

This is an achievement for the people of Alcester to cherish, and one worth guarding with the utmost zealousness.

A celebration of a different kind: an air-raid shelter is unceremoniously demolished in the High Street at the end of the Second World War

Index

Italicized page numbers denote illustrations